The
NATURE
REMEDY

HQ

The Nature Remedy

A restorative guide to the natural world

FAITH DOUGLAS

HQ
An imprint of HarperCollins*Publishers* Ltd
1 London Bridge Street
London SE1 9GF

This edition 2020

1
First published in Great Britain by
HQ, an imprint of HarperCollinsPublishers Ltd 2020

Faith Douglas asserts the moral right to be identified as the author of this work.
A catalogue record for this book is available from the British Library.

ISBN: 978-0-00-833197-9

Page design and typesetting by Emily Voller
Printed and bound by GPS Group

MIX
Paper from
responsible sources
FSC C007454
FSC
www.fsc.org

This book is produced from independently certified FSC™ paper
to ensure responsible forest management.

For more information visit: www.harpercollins.co.uk/green

To my children:
Owen, Freya, Elliot and Lilith

'Those who contemplate
the beauty of the Earth find
reserves of strength that will
endure as long as life lasts.'

RACHEL CARSON,
AUTHOR AND CONSERVATIONIST

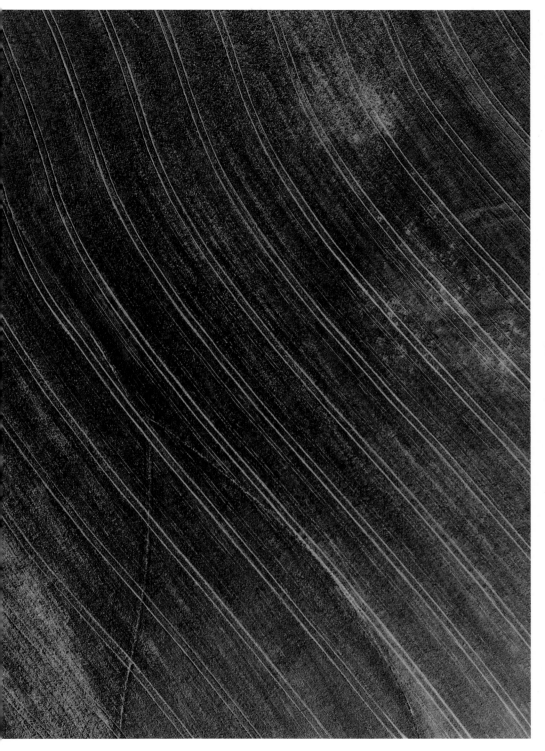

DISCOVERING THE HEALING POWER OF NATURE

Somewhere along the way, I found myself going through a very difficult time. I was trying to manage my professional life and my family life, and at the same time I was experiencing domestic abuse. I didn't really realise it was domestic abuse at first, or that it could be happening to me, but it did happen and it can happen to anyone. The most important thing is that I got out, I survived – and I feel I have the natural world to thank for my resilience and recovery.

After ending the relationship, I was continually stalked and terrorised for a number of months. Eventually, with help from the police and IDAS (Independent Domestic Abuse Services), my abuser was imprisoned and protections were put in place to keep me safe. However, the fear had been incredibly real and overwhelming. I was also working with the charity Help for Heroes at the time and this experience, combined with my nursing background, meant I was all too aware of the signs that I had developed post-traumatic stress disorder (PTSD). I knew what I needed to do. I threw myself into my work and took sanctuary in my home and the surrounding countryside. I practised mindfulness and experienced first-hand the benefits that a natural environment can have on somebody's emotional, mental and physical health.

At some point during this time, the term 'forest bathing' appeared in my life. There was little information available about this practice back then, which had roots in Japan, so I started to do some research into it. The practice made sense and came naturally to me. It clearly worked and the great thing was that science backed up everything I was experiencing.

I started to share the benefits of forest bathing with other people. I set up forestbathing.uk as there was nothing else like it at the time in Britain, and I wanted to show people just how easy and obvious this stuff was, and to enable people to take responsibility for their own wellbeing. I now run retreats, workshops and walks for people from many different backgrounds, young and old, all around the country. Everyone can improve their lives using nature – it's fun, it's free and it's easy. You can read more on forest bathing on page 114.

NATURAL PRECEPTS TO LIVE BY

The more people I meet, the more individuals I come across who are crying out for a connection with the natural world. Today, society is in many ways dangerously disconnected – people are separate both from each other and their surroundings. Mental health problems and stress are on the rise for children and adults. We need nature; we are part of it and the sooner we embrace the natural element in our lives, the sooner balance will be restored in our lives. Ultimately, I believe this will lead to balance in the environment itself.

Today, I live by a number of precepts, which have given my own life calm and meaning. Why not bring these into your life, too, and see what magic happens?

GO OUT INTO NATURE EVERY DAY
This could be a walk in the park or the walk to work; it could just mean stepping outside your front door or opening your window to breathe. Simply allow yourself to 'be' in nature.

EVERY DAY BE MINDFUL IN NATURE
Switch on your senses, listen and look at your surroundings. Let everything else melt away and feel that relief – even if just for a moment.

EVERY DAY SAY THANK YOU TO NATURE
To have gratitude for something to which we are so deeply connected brings an appreciation for all life like no other.

HAVE FAITH IN NATURE AND MAKE NATURE A HABIT

THE NATURE OF THIS BOOK

This book builds upon these key precepts in five chapters. The subject in each chapter is enormous in scope and could potentially fill whole libraries, so I've focused on topics that I hope will tickle your curiosity and encourage you to find out more about those areas that interest you.

Throughout these pages you will find tips, exercises, journaling prompts and suggestions for ways to enjoy an urban detox that will enhance your connection with the natural world. Feel free to experiment: what works for one person won't necessarily work for another; nature is fluid, changing effortlessly and accepting what is without judgement, so if you follow this approach you won't go far wrong.

If you read *The Nature Remedy* from cover to cover many times over, something different could resonate with you when it is most needed, or you could simply dip into it any time you need a reminder of your connection with nature or some respite from your daily worries. Lend it to a friend and pass it around: to share is to care.

21 DAYS OF NATURE

Why not make nature a healthy habit? We spend so much of our lives developing habits and behaviours by repeatedly carrying out the same tasks, day in and day out. Keep a note of your connection in nature for twenty-one days and see what happens – see how quickly it becomes a natural part of your everyday life.

JOURNALING

Journaling is an ancient technique that is probably as old as handwriting itself. The ancient Japanese journaled some 2,000 years ago. Today, many people continue to find journaling immensely therapeutic. It's a process that allows you to express all your thoughts and feelings without judgement and can provide a great sense of release.

Journaling has so many benefits, it:

- Encourages a state of mindfulness;
- Is a great stress-reliever;
- Can help you to achieve your goals;
- Boosts confidence and memory;
- Encourages creativity.

Throughout this book you will come across journal prompts and I would strongly encourage you to write down your thoughts, views and feelings in response to them. Buy or make a beautiful nature journal. Doodle and draw or stick things in it; make it your own personal journey through the wonders of the natural world – and see where it takes you …

A NATURAL REMINDER

Many years ago, I cut a ribbon from a book to wear on my wrist as a reminder of the importance of calm. When the ribbon wore thin, I replaced it with another, then another – and, along with keeping the copy of that book on my shelves, I still wear a ribbon reminder on my wrist today.

While there is no ribbon in this volume, it's easy to make a bookmark of your own. Then, when you reach the end of this book, you can either tie it around your wrist as a daily reminder of your connection to nature or place it in a picture frame and hang it where you will see it every day.

Gather at least eight long blades of fresh grass (the sturdy kind that grow in hedgerows or ornamentally are good options) and soak them in warm water to make the grass easier to work with.

Gather the blades together and tie a knot to secure them at one end.

Placing the knot at the top, secure the knot with a pin in a cork board or something similar to make it easier to weave.

Divide the blades into four sections, with two blades in each section.

Pick up the first section on the left, weave it up and over towards the right, until this section becomes the last section on the right.

Repeat with each section on the left, weaving it over to the right, and feeding in more grass as necessary, tightening it into place, until the bookmark is the desired length.

Check the finished result fits around your wrist, then tie the end to the initial knot to create a loop for your wrist. Or simply tie a knot in the end to create one long woven bookmark. You can trim any loose ends with scissors or attach a wooden bead to finish, securing with a knot.

HOW AWARE ARE YOU OF NATURE IN YOUR LIFE?

. . . .

. . . .

. . . .

HOW MUCH TIME DO YOU SPEND OUTDOORS?

. . . .

. . . .

. . . .

WHAT ARE YOUR THOUGHTS AND FEELINGS ABOUT THE NATURAL WORLD AND WHERE DOES IT SIT IN YOUR LIFE?

. . . .

. . . .

. . . .

WHAT IS YOUR HABITAT?

. . . .

. . . .

. . . .

The Sky & the Earth

1

The natural world is truly amazing: it supports our very existence. Our connection to it is quite simple, really, starting with the sky above our heads and the Earth beneath our feet. It can be all too easy to miss the wonder that surrounds us.

'The sky is the source of light in nature – and governs everything.'

JOHN CONSTABLE, ARTIST

THE SKY

I sometimes wonder how often people actually look up or take in more than what's right in front of their eyes. Even in the arboretum where I work, there are visitors who walk around with their heads down and their faces lit up by the screens of their phones. During my tours and talks, I find myself saying 'look up' a lot of the time, until it's almost become my personal mantra. You see, I think there is so much that can be missed above our heads, especially in an arboretum teeming with wildlife, interesting foliage, fruits, cones and berries: there's a whole other world going on up there.

THE EARTH'S ATMOSPHERE

If just for a moment we were able to expand our view, to look further than the branches of the trees, and rise up and up to where the birds fly high and balloons disappear, we would enter a realm we only usually experience through the window of an aeroplane (or when skydiving, if you're brave enough). The atmosphere that surrounds our planet consists of thin layers or blankets, each made up of gases that enable life on Earth. The atmosphere protects the Earth from the Sun's rays, allows the rain to fall and holds the oxygen we need to breathe. In short, the atmosphere enables life on our planet to exist.

If you were to jump into your car, set the cruise control to 70 mph and travel upwards for about an hour in a straight line you would be through the Earth's atmosphere and into space.

This atmosphere is made up of the following main layers:

IONOSPHERE

This changeable layer overlaps the Mesosphere, the Thermosphere and the Exosphere. It gets larger and smaller depending on how much energy it has absorbed from the Sun. This is the layer where auroras are formed; particles from the Sun and atoms from this layer collide to create the stunning rivers of coloured light in the sky that are visible near the North and South Poles.

EXOSPHERE

This outermost layer is about as wide as the Earth itself. While not much is known about this mysterious layer, the air here is very thin and temperatures can vary wildly from extremely hot to extremely cold. However, although the air may be very hot, it doesn't transmit much heat because it is so thin.

THERMOSPHERE

As there are relatively few molecules and atoms in this layer, absorbing even small amounts of solar energy can significantly increase the air temperature here, making the thermosphere the hottest layer in the atmosphere, where temperatures can reach 4,500 F, which is about 2,500 C. This layer is also home to the International Space Station that orbits our planet.

MESOSPHERE

In this middle layer, the temperature decreases to around -90°C. This is where meteors burn up due to friction caused by gases.

STRATOSPHERE

This vital layer is where the ozone sits, which absorbs the harmful ultraviolet radiation from the Sun and protects us here on Earth.

TROPOSPHERE

We live in this lowest layer. 'Tropos' is Greek for change, and this layer gets its name from the ever-changing weather systems that sit here. It contains the air we need to breathe, which is formed of 21 per cent oxygen, 78 per cent nitrogen and a 1 per cent blend of gases such as argon and carbon dioxide. It's nitrogen that creates the perfect conditions for life to form: this colourless gas is the building block for DNA and the proteins that both animals and plants require to grow, reproduce and survive. This layer also holds the water that creates clouds, rain and snow.

THE HEALING BREATH

For humans, the most important ingredient in the wondrous mixture of air is, of course, life-giving oxygen, which enters the body with each breath we take. With around thirty trillion cells in our body needing oxygen, our breath really is our life.

While we often take breathing for granted, I know from personal experience as an asthma sufferer what it's like not to be able to breathe. Some of my earliest memories are of the panic of struggling to take in as much oxygen as possible – and it's exhausting. As the mother of two premature babies, I have also experienced sitting for hours and watching my children fight for each breath they took. I have held my own breath as my babies struggled to take theirs. Since discovering meditation and mindfulness, I have learned how to be aware of and control my breathing, which has had a huge and positive effect on my life.

Many meditation practices encourage us to breathe consciously through the nose, whose hairs and mucus act as a filter against pollutants, bacteria and disease. The nose also produces nasal nitric oxide, which is vital for the relaxation of the inner muscles of our blood vessels, which in turn increases blood flow, aids circulation and decreases blood pressure.

Breathing has an enormous effect on our entire nervous system and when we breathe correctly – relaxed and steadily through the nose, all the way down into our abdomen and our diaphragm – we trigger our vagus nerve, which connects the rest of our body to our brain.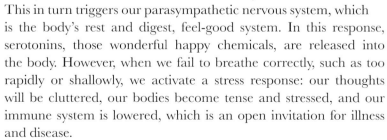
This in turn triggers our parasympathetic nervous system, which is the body's rest and digest, feel-good system. In this response, serotonins, those wonderful happy chemicals, are released into the body. However, when we fail to breathe correctly, such as too rapidly or shallowly, we activate a stress response: our thoughts will be cluttered, our bodies become tense and stressed, and our immune system is lowered, which is an open invitation for illness and disease.

According to ancient traditions, breathing correctly generates life energy. In Indian culture, this energy is known as prana, while the Chinese call it qi or chi.[1] Ancient Indian culture also used to measure the human lifespan in breaths rather than years. On average we take ten million breaths a year (which would make me about 420 million breaths old – I am not sure if I'm fascinated or horrified by how old that makes me sound!)

The breath remains a major focus for many types of meditation, and can be used as a way to control thoughts, emotions, discomfort and pain. Certain emotions cause certain types of breathing; for example, when we experience grief, our breath is short and shallow. Anger causes erratic breathing when we are more likely to breathe through our mouths, while anxiety causes us to breathe in a fast, short, shallow motion with our breath sitting high up in the lungs.

In contrast, deep, slow breathing into the abdomen will bring about calm, happy, relaxed feelings and help break the cycle of stress. Meditation and mindfulness can bring about this breathing response and with practice this quickly becomes a healthy, beneficial habit.

You see, our breath is amazing: we breathe on average between 20,000 and 30,000 times per day. However, most of us are unaware of our breath and have a tendency to breathe shallowly from high up in our chest, which means we only actually breathe to about 75 per cent of our full capacity. This can easily be increased with exercise and breathing techniques.

BELLY BREATHING

How many breaths have you been aware of today?
Belly breathing is a great way to become more aware of your
breath and increase your lung capacity.

Start by sitting comfortably. Allow yourself to relax with your hands
placed on your stomach.

Take some slow, deep breaths in through your nose.
See if you can fill your hands with your expanding stomach.

Now breathe out through your nose, emptying your lungs.

Next, slow your in-breath by inhaling for a count of five. Hold the
breath for a couple of counts before exhaling fully for a count of
five if possible. To complete the cycle, hold your breath again for a
count of two when your lungs are empty.

Repeat this process several times.

BLUE SKY THOUGHTS

As well as breathing deeply and slowly, simply watching the sky can be relaxing. I often find myself contemplating the big questions in life while gazing up above me, taking in life-giving air. Maybe it's because of the pure expanse of the space above, maybe it's the tranquillity and peace that sky gazing gives me.

While my head's in the clouds, I like to marvel at the colour of the sky above. On a bright day, it's the most beautiful blue, which makes me feel alive, warm and happy (actually, it's the same colour as my kitchen walls – I like to bring the outside world in).

When the light from the Sun reaches our Earth's atmosphere, it's scattered in all directions by the particles and gases in the air. Blue light is scattered further than other colours as it travels in shorter and smaller waves than they do. This explains why we see those wonderful blue-coloured skies on cloud-free days.

While we can see blue in the middle of the day, the reds, oranges and purples of a stunning gorgeous sunrise or sunset are created when the Sun is lower in the sky, which means that the Sun's light passes through much more of the atmosphere. Even more blue light is scattered, which allows the reds, yellows and oranges to pass through so we can see them.

Or can we? According to science, everybody's colour vision could vary and some research has gone so far as to suggest that one person's blue could be another person's red.[2]

BLUE SKY MEDITATION

There is a Tibetan meditation practice called blue sky gazing, which comes from the Dzogchen Buddhist tradition of teachings. These focus on discovering and continuing in the natural primordial state of being. It is believed that by gazing into the clear blue sky our minds will become clear and open, just like the sky above us. In the same way that the sky is unaffected by the passing weather, it is said that our minds too can be unaffected by our passing thoughts or feelings if we can reach this higher path.

Lie on your back outside, ideally with an expanse of clear sky overhead.

Take a few moments to calm your mind by taking some slow, deep breaths.

Gaze softly at the sky.

Each time your mind wanders, gently focus back on the in-breath and the out-breath.

Notice your in-breath and how it dissolves into the space inside you.

See your thoughts as passing clouds, and let them drift past.

Each time you follow the breath out, notice how it dissolves into the space outside you.

Keep following the in-breath and out-breath as they dissolve in the inner space and the outer space as part of the same cycle.

Notice how the inner space of the mind and the outer space of your being are exactly the same: the inner space is at one with the outer space.

CLOUD GAZING

While I appreciate the beauty of a clear blue sky, I also enjoy gazing upon skies full of fluffy white clouds. Even as an adult, I like to spend time cloud gazing, and I love listening to my children's wild imaginations when they join me, spotting the different fluffy shapes in the sky, watching how they move and change into different forms and shapes as if by magic.

Clouds are made up from water droplets or ice crystals and form when moist, cold air rises. At the point that the air cannot hold all of the water vapour in it, small light droplets or crystals create cloud. According to the World Meteorological Organisation's International Cloud Atlas, there are over a hundred different types of cloud. These can be grouped into ten basic types depending on their shape and where they sit in the sky:

1. **CUMULUS** These white fluffy clouds develop on a clear sunny day and bob around in blue sky like *The Simpsons'* clouds.

2. **STRATUS** These line the sky on dull, overcast days. They usually come with drizzle and fog – and that gloomy feeling.

3. **STRATOCUMULUS** Formed when cumulus join together to create a patchwork of cloud in the sky; these can be white or grey in colour.

4. **ALTOCUMULUS** Often mistaken for stratocumulus, these clouds sit higher up in the atmosphere. To tell the difference, place your hand up to the sky towards the cloud: if it's thumb-sized, it's altocumulus; if it's more of a fist size, it's stratocumulus.

5. **NIMBOSTRATUS** Dark grey in colour and usually blocking out the Sun, these are rain clouds.

6. **ALTOSTRATUS** This forms a sheet of cloud that covers the sky but which is thin enough to see the Sun through. These usually form ahead of a warm day.

7. **CIRRUS** The little fluffy, wispy clouds that you see on a fine warm day.

8. **CIRROCUMULUS** What we call in our family 'bits and bats' cloud, these small patches of cloud form high up and are 'cloudlets'.

9. **CIRROSTRATUS** A thin veil that appears when the atmosphere is full of moisture, these clouds can create a halo effect around the Sun or the Moon.

10. **CUMULONIMBUS** These huge clouds are generally darker at the bottom and they rise up high. These are thunderstorm clouds and generally a sign of severe weather. (These clouds generate a huge amount of excitement and energy within our family, with the thought of a good dramatic storm approaching.)

REMEDY

CLOUD APPRECIATION

While cloud gazing is a popular pastime in our family, so is cloud spotting, which led me to discover the Cloud Appreciation Society. This society was formed in 2005 by Gavin Pretor-Pinney to spread appreciation for these cotton-wool wonders, and now has over 46,000 members worldwide.[3] Their interesting website features a cloud of the month and a range of amazing cloud photos, poems and artwork.

Why not make cloud appreciation part of your life, too? On the first and last days of every month, and whenever you spot a spectacular sunrise or sunset, take a photograph of the clouds in the sky until you have captured the whole year.

THE SUN

I love sitting in my garden when the Sun is shining, regardless of the temperature – if it's a cool autumnal day I'll still sit outside, but with a few more layers on than normal. Even on a working day, I've been known to take my laptop outside to soak up every bit of sunshine possible, and though I often find myself battling with the sunlight on the screen in front of me, I think it's worth it.

The Sun is around 4.6 billion years old and sits at the heart of our solar system. Unlike Earth and the other large celestial bodies that form our solar system, the Sun isn't actually a planet; it's a star – a huge hot burning ball of hydrogen and helium. About a million Earths could fit inside the Sun as it's so vast, while the temperature of the part of the Sun that we can see is 5,500°C. The ultraviolet radiation that the Sun gives off is harmful to all living things and it's what causes us sunburn. However, solar heat is necessary for life to survive on Earth, while sunlight itself is a source of vitamin D.

Vitamin D is essential for keeping our bones and teeth healthy, supporting the function of our heart and lungs and the health of our brain, nervous system and immune system. As humans, we can get some of our vitamin D from our diet, but the most natural and effective way is from the Sun through our bare skin. While there are a number of factors that affect the amount of vitamin D that the human body makes from sunlight – such as location in the world, time of day, skin colour and how much skin is exposed – you don't need to risk getting sunburnt to acquire vitamin D, as it can take as little as 15 minutes outside for a fair-skinned person to make the necessary amount.

There has been an increase in people suffering from vitamin D deficiency in recent years and I do wonder if this is an effect of this technological age of ours; with people spending much more time indoors and less time outside, it's little surprise that it's affecting our health. During my last pregnancy I was surprised to find that it was expected that I would take vitamin D supplements as a matter of course. I declined, as I spend a great deal of my life outside and I am now very aware of how much time my youngest children spend outdoors too.

After a day at school or nursery, we often walk the dogs through the woods or we make time for a ride on our bikes. Our family week-ends are spent mostly outside regardless of the weather, be it by the side of a rugby pitch cheering on the team, chopping wood, doing chores or going on an adventure somewhere new. Even when my youngest, Lilith, was a tiny baby she had many of her naps outside in the garden either in my arms or wrapped in a blanket and laid on the grass. In Scandinavian countries, it's a tradition to leave babies outside to nap as this is believed to aid the child's sleep patterns and promote good health.[4] These infants are wrapped up in appropriate clothing and doze quite happily in sub-freezing temperatures.

Given the Sun's life-giving properties, it is little wonder that humans have worshipped the Sun from the dawn of time itself.

Cultures all over the world have traditionally worshipped the Sun, with the summer solstice often being revered as a peak time of the year for growth and abundance. In the Northern Hemisphere, the summer solstice takes place on around 21 June, marking the time of the year when the Sun is at its highest point in the sky. The word 'solstice' is taken from the Latin *sol* meaning 'sun', and *sistere*, meaning 'to stand still'.

In the UK, the summer solstice is one of the best times to visit Stonehenge. This stone circle was built around 3100 BCE, and while the reasons behind its construction remain largely unknown, the astronomer Sir Norman Lockyer pointed out that the north east axis aligns with the sunrise at summer solstice, which led to conjecture that the builders of the henge were perhaps Sun worshippers.[5] Today Stonehenge is still the focal point for many modern-day druids and pagans at important seasonal festivals such as the two annual solstices.

Elsewhere in the world, the ancient Egyptians aligned the great pyramids with the Sun and worshipped the Sun god Ra, who was said to be the ruler of the heavens and the bringer of light. Ancient Greeks similarly worshipped the Sun god Helios, who was said to ride a giant golden chariot pulled by winged horses across the skies, with which he towed the Sun. In Native American traditions, a sun dance was often performed not only to honour the Sun but also to bring about healing for the tribe and visions for the dancers. A sun dance could last for a number of days and was a test of a young warrior's endurance: a tree would be felled, decorated and painted and stood up at the site of the dance, the tribe would then paint their bodies and dance around the pole to sacred chanting and drum beats.

Today, I suppose the deckchairs you see lining the beach or around a pool could be seen as a form of Sun worship, too!

Given how important the weather is to us, it's perhaps no surprise that there are popular folk sayings about the Sun and sky. One that we often quote in our family is still used by many others today:

'Red sky at night,
shepherd's delight.
Red sky in the morning,
shepherd's warning.'

Another variation is:

'Pink sky at night,
sailor's delight.
Pink sky in the morning,
sailors take warning.'

However, the oldest version of this phrase is found in the Bible, Matthew 16:2–3

'When it is evening, you say,
"It will be fair weather;
for the sky is red."
And in the morning,
"It will be stormy today;
for the sky is red and threatening."'

COLOUR THERAPY

From the blues of clear skies to the golden colours of the Sun and the greens of the landscape, our natural world is ablaze with colour. When we slow down and take the time to really look, we might be surprised at just how much colour there is; the more you look, the more you notice. I often tell my groups at the arboretum that the grass isn't just green; we need to linger longer to notice all the different shades in it.

Going back through history, many cultures have used colour as a form of healing treatment. In fact, ancient Egyptian scrolls dating back to 1550 BCE were found to contain evidence of colour being used to heal ailments, while ancient Chinese texts also reveal that colour was used as a cure.

If we look at the colours of our natural world, we can apply them to a holistic therapy called chromotherapy which works with the effects that colour has on our minds and bodies:

THE BLUE OF THE SKY AND THE SEA
This colour brings about calm and serenity, is relaxing for the body and mind and lowers blood pressure and heart rate.

THE GREEN OF THE LANDSCAPE
Green is about comfort; also important for growth and renewal, it is said to be beneficial for our heart, lungs and circulation.

THE YELLOW OF THE SUN
This colour promotes happiness, can stimulate our minds and have a detoxing effect.

THE RED AND ORANGE OF THE SUNRISE AND SUNSET
Red is a passionate and warm colour that energises us, while orange also radiates warmth and promotes happiness.

THE NIGHT SKY

What about the sky at night? I don't know anyone who isn't impressed by the sight of a Full Moon. In the parkland where I live there is little light pollution and it can be pitch black at night at times, but during a Full Moon on a clear night, everything is lit up and we love going out – be it to walk the dogs, pop the chickens to bed or simply to look up and marvel at our wonderful skies.

The Moon and our Earth exist in perfect sync with each other, so much so that we can only ever see the same side of the Moon from Earth and we need to use a spacecraft to observe its dark side.

PHASES OF THE MOON

The Moon has eight different phases, which have influenced human behaviour for thousands of years. A great example of this is our calendar, in which a month is roughly equal to a Moon cycle of 28 days The phases are as follows:

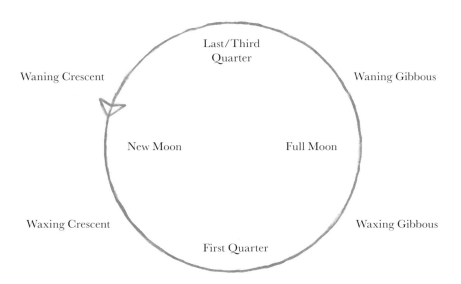

These phases are still used today in lunar gardening and have been acknowledged as long as agriculture itself has existed.[6] While some may see this approach as being based in mere superstition, there is some solid science to back it up.

The Moon and the Sun affect the Earth's gravitational pull. With a gravitational pull of its own, the Moon has an impact on the Earth's seas and causes rises and falls in sea levels that we know as tides. As the Moon pulls at the tides, it also pulls on the moisture content in the Earth and this in turn encourages growth. Scientific tests have shown that seeds planted at the Full Moon soak up greater amounts of water than during other phases. It's also been found that the Full Moon is good for root growth, while the Waxing Moon is the ideal time to cut lawns and to harvest, prune and fertilise crops.

LUNAR LORE

The Moon is unsurprisingly the centre of many mysteries, magic and superstitions. It is, for instance, thought to be lucky to expose a newborn baby to a Waxing Moon and lucky if a Full Moon falls upon a Moon day or Monday. However, it is said to be unlucky to see a Full Moon on a Sunday and unlucky to sleep exposed to the light of the Full Moon.

That said, I have also heard that it's energising to sleep in the light of a Full Moon, so I often sleep with the curtains open during a this lunar phase to test this theory. While I'm not really sure of the impact, I do know I love the sight of the Full Moon shining through our windows, as its brightness lights up the whole room.

'It is a beautiful and delightful sight to
behold the body of the Moon.'

**GALILEO GALILEI,
NATURAL PHILOSOPHER**

The Moon features in many myths – both classical and urban. In Greek mythology, Selene was the Moon goddess who rode her Silver Moon chariot across the skies, while in Roman mythology the Moon goddess was called Luna. 'Luna' is the Latin word for Moon from which our word lunatic is taken, and was originally used to describe someone who was believed to go crazy at the different phases of the Moon.

The Moon has long been blamed for the behaviour of both people and animals, and although there is no scientific evidence to support this theory, I have to say that during my nursing career we did witness changes of behaviour among patients at the Full Moon. We often found that people's sleep was poor during this phase and, of course, they were more likely to be agitated when sleep deprived.

A sleep study was carried out in which the participants slept in windowless rooms and they were still found to have sleepless nights during a Full Moon, so moonlight wasn't an explanation to this unsolved mystery. Humans are made up of 60 per cent water and we already know that the Moon affects the water in our seas, perhaps the Moon does have some kind of effect on us after all.

CATCH A SHOOTING STAR

On clear nights, my family and I often stargaze.
We have spent many an evening dragging blankets
and rugs outside with us, and lying on them until we
get too cold or too sleepy, just to watch the stars under
our massive parkland sky. If you don't have to worry about
getting children to bed early, it's best to go out when the night
is at its darkest between midnight and 4 a.m. Then it's usually a
bit of a competition to see who can spot the most shooting stars.
It's never long before we see the first one and the excitement builds
from there.

There are a number of meteor showers that make their way annually through Earth's atmosphere, which give us a great opportunity
to spot shooting stars. Our family favourite is the Perseids meteor
shower, which takes place around 11 August each year, when the
evenings are usually warm and pleasant.

One of my fondest memories is of our first night on a camping trip
to the Lizard Peninsula, in Cornwall, when my family sat outside
our tent with my youngest son, Elliot, who was then aged nine.
There was clear sky above us, next to no light pollution, and the
stars that night were quite literally out of this world. We sat for
a long time together and spotted many shooting stars and Elliot's
excitement each time he witnessed one was utterly contagious.

My family and I also like to see if we can identify the difference
between planets and stars. Generally, the planets seem to be much
brighter and don't twinkle, whereas the stars do. This can often
trigger much debate as to whether there is actual twinkling occurring or not.

We once experienced great excitement in our back garden, sat around our fire pit, when we witnessed a long line of travelling lights. Had it not been early summer we would've been sure it was Santa on his sleigh. As it was, we were convinced we had witnessed a UFO of some description. The next day I decided to google the event and sure enough, our 'Santa' was all over the internet. There had been a launch of sixty satellites the day before, and our excitement turned to disappointment, then to a sense of sadness, with the realisation that even the space above our heads isn't free from humans and all our stuff.

THE ANCIENT ART OF ASTRONOMY

The evidence suggests that astronomy is the oldest natural science. Dating to *c.*1600 BCE and discovered in modern-day Germany, the Nebra sky disk is made of bronze inlaid with images of the Moon, Sun and stars. It is believed that as well as being a religious object, this archaeological discovery may be an astronomical instrument. Native-American rock drawings dating from the same period have similarly been found to contain images of the skies above.

The Greeks and Romans were responsible for identifying most of the star constellations that we know today and naming them after mythological characters. The roots of much of their knowledge lay in the teachings of the ancient Babylonians, who not only created a calendar based on the Sun and the Moon phases but also devised zodiac or star signs in an age when astronomy was not seen as separate from astrology.

Our relationship with the stars goes back much further than this, though, with the discovery that we humans are essentially made up of star dust. Scientifically speaking, most of the elements that make up the human body were formed in stars billions of years ago. The six main elements that support our life – oxygen, hydrogen, nitrogen, carbon, sulphur and phosphorus – are found abundantly throughout the Milky Way. So we really are the stuff of stars.[7]

STARS AS NAVIGATION TOOLS

Stars have been used throughout history as natural navigational aids. While sailors could follow the coast line when close to land and refer to the directions of the eastern sunrise and western sunset during the daylight hours, night navigation was different. This was when they used the night sky like a huge map.

This is something that you can try for yourself by finding the North Star, also known as Polaris, which will always signpost you to the north. Start by looking for the constellation known as Ursa Major, also called the Plough or the Big Dipper. Some people even call it the Saucepan as it is an easily identified group of seven stars in the shape of a pan. Next, look for the pointer stars: if it were a real saucepan and you were about to pour it, the two pointer stars are on the side where the contents would come out. The North Star is exactly five times the distance between these two stars in the direction leading up and away from the pan. True north is the point just below the North Star.

GIVE A GIFT OF THE SKY

REMEDY

A night sky map makes a wonderful gift for a special occasion. I bought one for my other half to mark the time when we first met. It's a beautiful picture of the night sky as it appeared over our heads on that exact day. Whatever the reason – a birth, wedding or other memorable event – a night sky chart makes a special memento, capturing the heavens themselves.[8]

THE EARTH

Let's take our head out of the clouds now and bring our gaze back down to the ground beneath our feet. Have you ever thought about the Earth as being any more significant than the ground you're standing on? It is so much more than just a surface for us to stick to. It's our land, our planet, our spacecraft in our solar system, our home.

Scientists believe that leftover gases from the nebula that created the Sun formed our Earth around 4.5 billion years ago. The wonderful green and blue globe that we are lucky enough to share with millions of other different species of life hasn't always been able to support life. To begin with, the Earth was molten due to extreme volcanic activity. Over time, its surface cooled and hardened, and condensed water formed clouds and rain – then the oceans were created. Over hundreds of millions of years, the Earth's surface changed and land formed, creating a huge supercontinent which then split in two and again broke up and shifted to create what we now know as our continents today.

There are nearly nine million different species living on Earth at the moment and around seven billion people make up just one of those species. Given we are supposed to be the most intelligent life form on the planet, you would think we would recognise that we need to take care of the wonderful world we live on. But I often think that many people have forgotten just how connected we are to our life-giving planet.

I sometimes consider humans to be the biggest pest on Earth and wonder if without us here the planet would heal, nature would thrive and balance would be restored. However, I don't think anyone could say what would actually happen, given the damage we've done. But I like to think that nature knows the answers.

Many cultures, both ancient and modern, have referred to our planet as Mother Earth. The ancient Greeks knew Mother Earth as Gaea, who both represented the Earth and was the mother of the whole universe. In Greek mythology, she gave birth to gods and humans. Native North American cultures have a wonderful saying that I love: 'Beneath the clouds lives the Earth Mother from whom is derived the water of life, who at her bosom feeds plants, animals and humans.'

Everything we need to survive and thrive is given to us by the Earth, by Mother Nature. Although the rise of industry and technology is increasingly distancing us from the natural world, the basics of life – food, water, medicine and shelter – are provided free of charge in nature.

REMEDY

CELEBRATE EARTH HOUR

Founded in 2007, Earth Hour is a wonderful event during which communities worldwide come together to pledge their support to our planet, our Earth, simply by switching off lights.[9]

It's very easy to take part, and you can participate in Earth Hour in your own way. We as a family show our support by spending the hour in candlelight with absolutely everything, not just the lights, switched off.

How about getting your local community together and plunging the street you live in into magical candlelight for an hour? Or involve your local school, which will combine a little bit of excitement at the event with an important message of giving something back to our planet.

THE NATURE OF THE EARTH

The Earth has multiple layers. At its very centre, its core consists of two parts that are mostly made up of iron. The inner core is solid while the outer core is molten with a temperature to rival the Sun's surface. The next layer is the Earth's mantle, a thick layer of silicate rock that divides the core and the crust. The crust is the Earth's thinnest layer and could be likened to the skin of an apple in comparison to the other layers, being only about 3 to 5 miles thick under the oceans and around 25 miles thick under land, where it is deepest in mountainous regions.

The outer layer of the Earth's land crust is made up of sedimentary rock consisting of crushed particles made from stone, dead plants and animals. Over time this layer will eventually include our own remains, which really does tell us just how much of a part we play in the make up of this planet.

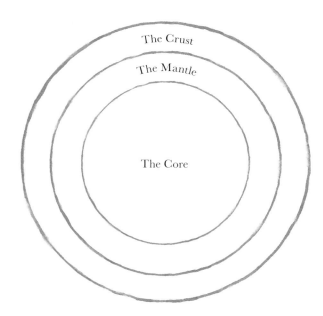

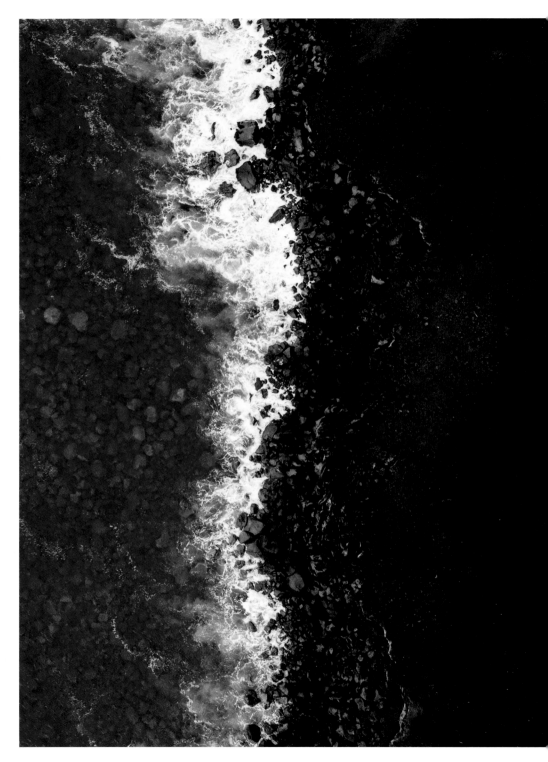

OUR PRECIOUS OCEANS

With 70 per cent of the Earth's crust being covered in water at an average depth of around 2.5 miles, it's no wonder that we have only managed to explore 5 per cent of the ocean floor. In fact, we've managed to map more of the Moon, Venus and Mars than we have of these areas.

So much about the oceans remains a mystery to us, although we do know that these vast expanses of water are vital ecosystems. Not only are they life-givers to marine creatures but oceans are essentially the heart and lungs of the planet, providing us with half of the oxygen we breathe.

However, the oceans are showing signs of ill health caused by high levels of greenhouse gases, over-fishing, pollution and destruction in habitats. Symptoms including warming up, acidifying, changes in water circulation and huge dead zones lead in turn to major changes in marine ecosystems that result in less-abundant coral reefs, fewer small fish, breakdowns in food chains and more frequent pests and diseases. It's cause for concern.

Given all this water on our planet and in our oceans, it's eye-opening to discover that 97 per cent of the water is unusable, with fresh water being quite scarce. Fresh water makes up only about 2.5 per cent of water on the planet, most of which is found in ice caps and glaciers, while the rest is ground water.

Water is a precious commodity, and even if we don't live by the ocean we can help to preserve it by changing our daily habits.

EVERYDAY BEACH CLEAN

The water we drink has been around in some form or another for millions of years and is continuously recycled. Given that most of us in the West can turn our taps on and water flows freely, I suspect most people don't really give much thought to it.

However, the global plastic crisis tells us that around twelve million tonnes of plastic now enter our oceans each year. Thankfully, it seems that many people today are taking our global plastic crisis seriously and there are lots of different workplaces and organisations that have gone plastic-free to try to make a difference.

This is something that you can also begin to do by, for example:

Switching from liquid shower gels and hand wash to solid soap bars in the bathroom.

Replacing kitchen roll with reusable dish cloths in the kitchen, and using recyclable glass jars for storage.

Using biodegradable plant pots rather than plastic in the garden.

Why not take a bit of time each month to research other ways to go plastic-free, and keep a note of any ideas in your journal, so that they begin to become a way of life?

THE HIDDEN MESSAGES OF WATER

The late Japanese scientist Dr Masaru Emoto is the author of the book *The Hidden Messages in Water*. In it, he argues that 'water is the blueprint of our reality' and proposes that emotional vibrations and energies can actually change the structure of water.

He found a way to photograph microscopic frozen water particles and his experiments revealed physical changes in the way a water particle appears after being exposed to certain types of conditions.[10] One of Dr Emoto's experiments was conducted with a class of school children, who were given three glasses of water. The rules were simple: they were to ignore one glass, speak kindly to another and be cruel to the last one.

His photographs of the water crystals after this experiment are amazing. The water crystals in the glass that was ignored formed an indistinct smudge-like image when photographed; the crystals in the glass that was told it was beautiful formed incredible snow-flake-like patterns; while the crystals in the glass that was called unkind things looked ugly.

REMEDY

DR EMOTO'S RICE EXPERIMENT

Dr Emoto's rice experiment can be easily replicated at home:

Take three identical clean jars.

Add equal amounts of cooked rice to each jar.

Measure and add equal amounts of water into
each jar – just enough to cover the rice.

Put a sticker on one jar saying:
'I love you.'

Put a sticker on another jar saying:
'I hate you.'

Leave the remaining jar blank.

Every day for thirty days, do the following:

Hold the jar that says 'I love you' on it and tell the
jar and its contents just how much you love it.

Hold the jar that says 'I hate you' on it and tell
this one just how much you hate it.

Completely ignore the jar with no sticker;
in fact turn your back on it.

**Why not give this simple experiment a go
and see what your findings are?**

If we were able to take pictures of the water particles in our bodies in the way that Dr Emoto did, what would they look like? Given we are mostly made up of water, could we be impacting on our own water particles with negative talk and harmful thought patterns? Some of the things we say to ourselves in our heads we wouldn't dream of saying to another person but for some reason we think it's all right to do so to ourselves.

What would you want your water particles to look like? I know I would like mine to form the most beautiful snowflake pattern – just like the one in the classroom experiment.

I have told Dr Emoto's story to my own children to encourage self-love as well as kindness to other living things. Occasionally this comes back to bite me when I am accused of damaging their water particles when they have to do something they may not necessarily want to do, like tidying a bedroom!

THE HEALING PROPERTIES
OF WATERFALLS AND
MOUNTAINS

One body of water that I am completely in awe of is the waterfall: I love the cascading, crashing water and the crisp, fresh spray in the air; there's something dream-like about them. Waterfalls are so much more than water purifiers; they are important for whole ecosystems, and have a positive impact on human health as well. Waterfalls release negative ions; these atoms and molecules occur naturally in air that has been charged with electricity and can have a direct effect on our wellbeing, helping us to feel calm. They also help to reduce stress and depression, and to purify our blood, improve cell metabolism and boost our immune system.

Negative ions do this by having a direct effect on the cells in our own bodies. Our cells are made up of atoms, which contain both negative and positive charges depending on the number of electrons or protons they carry. Most healthy atoms have a negative charge because they contain more electrons, but sometimes these healthy atoms can have electrons taken from them, leaving them in a damaged state. In this state, they are known as free radicals and can have a detrimental effect on our cells, which causes our health to decline, and we become susceptible to illness and disease. Our health can then decline, and we become susceptible to illness and disease. To help stop this destructive process, we can give ourselves large free doses of negative electrons from simple exposure to nature.

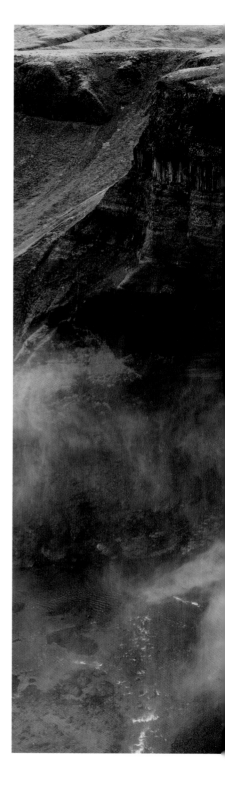

If we climb to the top of a waterfall and keep going high up into the mountains, we will reach the majestic peaks that were formed when pieces of the Earth's crust, called plates, crashed together and pushed the crust up into mountainous forms. The Himalayas were formed some fifty-five million years ago, and include thirty of the world's highest mountains, among them Mount Everest, with its summit being the highest point on Earth, at 8,850 metres.

While it's a dream of mine, I've never visited the Himalayas, although I have visited mountain ranges in the UK, Norway, Switzerland and North Africa. No matter how harsh the conditions I have experienced in these places, there is a special quality of peace to be found in a mountain range. It could be the achievement of getting there, the sprawling views if the weather allows it, or the buzz of adrenaline… but I think it's something more.

A mountain has a special solidness about it; its mighty stillness is breathtaking and the air, well, it's just unbelievable. Mountain air is so fresh and so pure, it even smells healthy. There is little pollution up in the mountains and I think our bodies know this. In fact, studies tell us that spending time around mountains is good for our health – our heart and respiratory systems are healthier and our stress levels decrease. It's been suggested that living in mountain ranges can increase our lifespan.[11]

FROM MOUNTAINS TO MUD

The Earth beneath our feet matters, from the highest mountain right down to the seemingly simple soil. I'm a horticulturalist by trade and I know how vital soil, is not just for plant life but for our own lives as well.

Healthy, fertile soil provides the nutrients for plants to grow, which in turn provide us with the oxygen we need to breathe. More than this, healthy soil recycles organic matter, purifies water and contains microbes that are good for us.

Today, our society's motto is often 'don't touch' – don't get dirty. But did you know that a little bit of mud under the fingernails is good for you? Research shows that soil contains antidepressant microbes. These wonderful microscopic bacteria are called *Mycobacterium vaccae* and have been found to have the same effect on our brains as antidepressant drugs do, but without the unpleasant side-effects. But it's not just about making skin contact from the soil; we also inhale these bacteria when we potter in our gardens, which raises our serotonin levels and makes us feel well and happy.[12]

'Walk as if you are kissing the Earth with your feet.'

**THICH NHAT HANH,
BUDDHIST MONK AND PEACE ACTIVIST**

EARTHING

Most of us live our lives with a constant barrier between us and the Earth, be that through flooring, transport or simply shoes. Yet a physical connection with our planet is important for our wellbeing. Going barefoot is thankfully an increasingly popular trend – and a healthy one.

I often lead barefoot walks with groups and I love being barefoot myself. However, many people can think it's a bit 'weird', and the sight of someone walking along barefoot may even raise questions of sanity in the West. But I ask you which is stranger – barefoot or stilettos? I know which I can walk in and which I can't.

We were born barefoot, and if you watch a child who's never worn shoes, the way in which they use their feet is amazing. My daughter Lilith was walking when she was one year old, however, as she had been a premature baby, her feet were tiny. We weren't able to get shoes small enough for her, so Lilith went barefoot for many months. It amazed me how she was never fazed by the surface underfoot and how she used her feet as so much more than merely a means to keep herself upright.

A study of children at a school in New Zealand, where they were barefoot 50 per cent of the time, both indoors and outdoors, found that their feet behaved differently; the big toe was often further apart from the rest of the toes to give support and aid balance (unlike our shoed feet where our toes are often squashed up together).[13] They walk differently; their gait is more organic and the movement more fluid as they use their hips much more freely.

There are wonderful health benefits to going barefoot. Like waterfalls, the Earth gives off negative ions, which we can soak up through skin contact like sponges. Grounding, or earthing as it is sometimes called, gives us a huge boost of antioxidants free of charge. It not only boosts our immune system but has been found to help us sleep better, help with pain and discomfort and balance cortisol levels, which in turn affects our stress response.

Often on the walks I lead, people are surprised at how warm the ground is and how refreshing contact with the damp ground can be. We not only walk through grass but through streams and in woodland to experience different textures. And I always like to show off a little by picking up pine cones with my toes and throwing them around!

I find the reactions from these groups amazing, and have watched people from all walks of life, who wouldn't usually dream of getting their feet dirty, be reduced to giggles as they tiptoe in almost a child-like manner around a woodland. It's a surprisingly mindful activity and when you put your shoes and socks back on afterwards you have the most amazingly fresh-footed feeling – it's almost as if your feet are shouting at you to remind you of the importance of that much-needed connection with our healing Earth.

GROUNDING

When was the last time you removed your shoes and socks and had a good old paddle around barefoot?

Perhaps it was on a sunny beach holiday.

How about giving grounding a go in your everyday life, either in a woodland, park or even in your own back garden?

Wherever there is grass, sand or soil, simply remove your shoes (socks are optional if the weather is a little chilly, as you will still get some benefits), and go for a wander. A recommended dose is thirty minutes a day to kickstart the body's natural healing process.

Experiment with different textures, play with your balance and give throwing a pine cone with your toes a go. If you want to make this a social activity, look at joining a guided barefoot walk or group.

There are other ways you can experience grounding:

Wear natural leather-soled shoes

Lie on the ground

Go wild swimming

Garden with your bare hands

Sit against a tree

HOW DO YOU BREATHE? DEEPLY, SHALLOWLY? QUICK OR
SLOW? HOW DOES YOUR BREATH AFFECT YOUR EMOTIONS,
OR CHANGE ACCORDING TO HOW YOU FEEL?

. . . .

. . . .

. . . .

WHAT ARE YOUR THOUGHTS AFTER SKY GAZING AND CLOUD GAZING?

. . . .

. . . .

. . . .

WHAT ARE YOUR FINDINGS IN THE RICE EXPERIMENT?

. . . .

. . . .

. . . .

HOW GROUNDED ARE YOU?

. . . .

. . . .

. . . .

Trees

2

Trees are one of my great passions and what I seek out whenever I want to ground myself and renew my connection with nature. In fact, I wrote most of this chapter while sitting underneath some of my favourite trees. Being among trees is where I feel at my most calm and relaxed, and where I find clarity.

I am lucky enough to call a woodland not only my home but my office. As I mentioned in the introduction, for the past decade or so I have been the curator of an arboretum, where I look after 100 acres of ancient and rare trees. My connection to nature has always been strong but during the time that I have worked in the arboretum, it has developed into a complete way of life that I am now fortunate to share with many other people.

'Let the beauty of what you love be what you do.'

RUMI, SUFI POET

I once got talking to a woman I met out walking among the trees, who explained to me that she had come to the arboretum to find peace and escape for a little while from her hectic life. She said that each time she went for a walk she went back home feeling like she had returned from holiday. This really stuck with me: the relief, the peace and support that these wonderful living giants provide is invaluable.

For me, trees are not only the lungs of the Earth, they are the very backbone of our planet.

A LIFE AMONG THE TREES

I discovered my own love of trees early on in life. I grew up in Harrogate, a beautiful tree-filled town, where I was lucky to have access to the town's most famous park, the Valley Gardens, and Pinewoods, with its ninety-six acres of woodland, which I used as my playground. My parents both worked hard and would often take my brother, me and our dog on long walks in the woods at the weekend or in the evening after dinner. This was always an adventure as we ran between the trees, spotting bats and listening to the owls.

I was obsessed with Enid Blyton's *The Magic Faraway Tree* and other books steeped in folklore and the magic of nature, and as my brother and I ran freely in the woods, so did our imaginations. I often dreamt of fairies and pixies living among the trees. I realise now how lucky I am that my parents chose such a healthy pastime for our family.

We sometimes went on holiday to Scotland, where we would stay in remote wooded places. To this day, one of my first and fondest childhood memories is of the swishing noise of the wind among tall pine trees. I now know that the sound of wind through leaves and branches is known as 'psithurism', the voice of the forest. It's also one of the many natural sounds to have a calming and relaxing effect on our minds.

My obsession with trees struck again when I was a teen-ager and my friends and I went through a stage of hanging out in the woods, drawn there by tales of magic and witch-craft. As an adult, I have always been fortunate to live close to wild spaces. During my nursing career, I would often sit under a tree after a long shift or take a woodland walk as a way of processing the day I'd had. Working in the arboretum spending time with trees each day, I think I may actually have the best job in the world.

Over the years, I've come to appreciate the love, wonder and connection that many other people feel for trees, and I am regularly asked for advice on how to save beloved trees from being cut down or how to help save sick ones. You only have to consider the public reaction to the Sheffield street tree crisis in recent years to see how deeply people care. The news that 17,500 trees were scheduled to be cut down in one of the UK's greenest cities saw people come together not just from Sheffield but from all over the country to save them, saddened and horrified that healthy trees were set to be removed for no good reason.

One interesting piece of information to emerge from this urban crisis was that a figure of around £37,000 was given for each mature tree left standing, to impress their importance upon those who are inclined to view them in monetary terms. The value of air conditioning, pollution removal, flood defence and erosion control, and wildlife habitats (not to mention the health benefits for us from phytoncides, the oils given out by trees) all adds up to confirm just how precious trees are.

'Whoever has learned how to listen to trees no longer wants to be a tree. He wants to be nothing except what he is. That is home. That is happiness.'

**HERMANN HESSE,
WRITER AND PAINTER**

SAVING AN OLD FAVOURITE

I was recently asked to give an interview about the horse chestnut tree, known to many as the conker tree. Many of us in Britain will have fond memories of autumns when our pockets were full of shiny brown conkers, seeing who could find the biggest. My own father would take my brother and I conkering; he would throw a stick up into a tree while we watched with delight as conkers fell to the ground, before rushing to collect the treasure. Today, I go conkering with my own children and even my toddler, Lilith, gets excited and carries a conker in each hand after they've fallen. I've even won a conker championship as an adult and it's one of my proudest moments: my name is on a cup in a village pub somewhere in Yorkshire and I still have the wrinkly, shrunken, winning conker displayed in the cabinet at home. My son Elliot keeps asking me for the secret to my success – which I'll never reveal.

Sadly, the much-loved horse chestnut tree has recently been classified as vulnerable to extinction and put on the IUCN (International Union for Conservation of Nature) red list in a report that states over half of Europe's native trees are now under severe threat.[14] A number of diseases and invasive pests attack the horse chestnut, including the leaf miner moth, the larva of which burrows and feeds on the leaves, covering them in brown patches. Eventually these leaves die and drop off, but although new leaves grow they are also affected and the condition stunts the tree's growth. Conkers from infected trees are noticeably smaller as well.

While it's thought that some birds, namely tits, feed on the larvae, with wild habitats being destroyed for smaller nesting birds at an alarming rate, it's no wonder pests like the leaf miner moth are ravaging the horse chestnuts in this country. However, it's not just pests and diseases that affect this wonderful tree: with only between 5,000 and 9,000 mature horse chestnuts left in all of Europe, it's been found that residential and commercial development presents the greatest danger to them, with farming, mining and logging also being significant factors in their decline.

It turns out that the very humans who love the conkers from these fantastic trees are, in fact, their greatest threat. In addition to campaigning to save individual trees, it's important to do what we can to rescue entire species. Trees are essential to the health of our living planet, and to our own wellbeing.

In addition to this, trees have provided mankind with valuable resources since time immemorial. Practically speaking, we have always used trees for energy – for firewood as fuel to keep us warm and cook food since Stone Age times, through to modern-day fossil fuels, which are formed from compressed forests beneath layers of earth. We use wood to build shelters and houses for us to inhabit; to make furniture, to build ships and musical instruments to entertain us.

As we will see later in this chapter, some of the healthiest foods come from trees (you can even drink some types of tree sap, such as maple syrup, walnut sap and birch sap), and the basis of many of our modern medicines and remedies originate from them as well.

CONKER SHAMPOO

Once you've finished playing a game of conkers, why not make your own conker shampoo?

20 horse chestnuts

1 small apple, sliced, with seeds

350 ml water

Old clean cloth, for straining

3 tablespoons of linseeds or flax seeds

1. Crush the chestnuts into small pieces and put them into a pan. Add the apple and water. (Apple is great for nourishing and moisturising hair.)

2. Bring to the boil, then cover the pan and simmer for 25 minutes.

3. Line a sieve or colander with an old cloth and strain the stock through it into another clean pan.

4. Now add the linseeds to the liquid as a thickening agent and stir until there are no lumps left.

5. Once cooled, pour the liquid into a clean airtight bottle, store in the fridge and use within a month of making.

WHAT IS A TREE?

If you were to look up the definition 'tree' in a dictionary, you might find a description such as:

> 'A woody, perennial plant with a
> single stem or trunk supporting
> branches and leaves.'

But they are much more fascinating than that. Trees are not only the tallest plants on Earth but also some of the oldest living entities. The largest trees include the giant redwoods (*Sequoiadendron giganteum*) found along the west coast of America. There is a giant redwood in the arboretum where I work; however, it's simply a baby at 250 years old, compared to the 3,000-year-old giants in California.

The largest trees I've ever seen grow in an arboretum in Belgium. These trees are around 100 years old and while they are only young in comparison to the ancient redwoods, they are already incredibly tall. They look to me as though they go through growth spurts, making them appear long and thin compared to similar trees in Britain. Reasons for this will be climate-based, while water levels also play a large part in determining their growth patterns.

Depending on the species, the average lifespan of a tree can range from forty or fifty years (for palm trees, for example) to 5,000 years, as in the case of the bristlecone pine (*Pinus longaeva*). However, trees regularly outlive their expected lifespans and with the average lifespan for a tree being 150 years in the UK, it's nice to know we still have some oldies standing. There are oaks that date back to medieval and Tudor times, with some of the oldest found to be over 1,000 years old. The oldest living tree in the UK is believed to be the Fortingall Yew, which stands in Perthshire, Scotland, and is thought to be between 2,000 and 3,000 years old. Could you imagine the stories these ancients could tell us?

Dendrology is the scientific study of trees and although our understanding of these incredible plants is continuously improving, there is still much we don't know about them – such as whether they feel pain. If we look at the basic biological makeup of a tree, we can see that they are consist of a canopy of leafy branches that connect to the main stem (or trunk), which leads to the vital root system underground.

A tree's leaves absorb carbon dioxide during photosynthesis, a process that transforms light energy from the Sun into chemical energy by means of chloroplasts, or plant cells, which, along with water, produces the food that enables a plant to survive and grow. Deciduous trees shed their leaves seasonally to take a rest from the process, and also shed them to adapt to extremes of cold or warm weather, while evergreens keep their leaves (or needles) throughout the year.

The inner bark then carries the carbon, or food, from the leaves down through the branches into the stem. Trees store carbon in their stem and branches; in fact, about 50 per cent of the dry mass of a tree is carbon.

The stem or trunk of a tree is made up of a protective layer of bark, which I like to think of as the tree's skin. The cambium sits beneath the bark and acts as a tissue layer that forms partially undifferentiated cells. The inner bark, which sits within the cambium layer, houses an entire vascular system that runs all around the tree, from its leaves to its roots, carrying food, nutrients and water.

HOW TO AGE A TREE

To accurately age a tree, you would need to count the growth rings in a cross section of its trunk, with each ring relating to a year of its life. This doesn't necessarily mean cutting the tree down; botanists can take core samples by inserting an instrument just over halfway into the tree's trunk and removing a sample, or core, of the inside of the stem. However, although this way of sampling is preferable to cutting a tree down, it can cause damage to trees.

I much prefer the tape measure option:

Measure the girth of the stem at shoulder height in centimetres, and then look up the growth factor for the type of tree you're measuring, which is how much width it gains annually. (For example, an oak will gain approximately 2 centimetres, while hazel, ash and beech will gain 2.5 centimetres and pine and spruce will gain 3.25 centimetres.) Then divide the girth measurement by the relevant growth figure to give an approximate age.

To age a conifer or evergreen, simply count the rows of branches that grow off the main stem (although you will need to add two to four years to this figure to allow for seedling growth).

The growth rings inside a tree trunk don't just reveal the age of that tree; they can inform us about the tree's growing conditions. Thick rings usually show there was plenty of light and water in a particular year, while thin rings suggest the opposite. They can also hold scars from damage and ill health.

WHY TREES ARE IMPORTANT

As part of the photosynthesis cycle, trees and other plants release oxygen into the air – oxygen that we humans breathe. Besides providing humans with such an essential resource, research has shown that trees remove pollution from the air,[15] which can help prevent human deaths from conditions such as acute respiratory disease. Given that the average human being inhales and exhales around 20,000 times a day, to breathe we need the oxygen supplied by around roughly seven or eight trees a year each. With over seven billion people on the planet, that's an awful lot of trees.

As deforestation is often in the news these days, I sometimes wonder if we have enough trees to ensure our future survival on this planet. Reports from Global Forest Watch, an organisation that uses satellite images from the World Resources Institute to monitor the decline in forests around the world, estimate that we lost around 72.6 million acres of rainforest in 2019. If we focus for a moment on the Amazon rainforest, 17 per cent of this vital ecosystem has been lost to deforestation in the last fifty years. With most of this being due to the encroachment of agriculture and around 18.7 million acres a year being lost to illegal logging, it presents a major concern.[16] However, we shouldn't forget that deforestation is a global issue.

AFRICA'S GREAT GREEN WALL

This African-led project dates back to the 1970s, when vast areas of previously fertile land in a region called the Sahel, spanning the southern edge of the Sahara Desert, started to become barren owing to the effects of climate change, population growth and unsustainable land management practices.[17] The aim is to grow an 8,000-kilometre natural wonder of trees and plants across the width of Africa. When the Great Green Wall is finished, it is set to be the largest living structure on the planet. The project is about 15 per cent complete and, as well as fighting climate change, communities are already benefitting from the return of food, jobs, security and life in this area.

BRITAIN'S FORESTS

For much of its prehistoric existence, the landmass that became modern Britain was predominately forest, with around 90 per cent tree coverage. From the earliest attempts at farming in 3,000 BCE onwards, there was a reduction in this percentage. This decline continued steadily and rapidly from the 1500s onwards with the emergence of modern Europe – right through to the beginning of the twentieth century, when the figure was all the way down to a shocking 7 per cent. Thanks to a combination of our modern-day need for sustainable timber supplies and the realisation of the damaging environmental effects of deforestation and the subsequent need to replant, we have managed to bring the percentage of wooded land back up to 13 per cent in the present day, which equates to roughly 3.19 million hectares.

However, compared to other countries in Europe, such as France with 31 per cent of woodland and Finland with 73 per cent, this is still not good enough. So what are we doing about it? Well, in comparison to countries such as China, which planted six million hectares of trees in 2019 – an area the size of Ireland – the UK is still not doing enough. But are we trying? The Woodland Trust charity has made it their mission not only to preserve what little woodland we have left but to plant more.[18] Over the next twenty-five years, over fifty million new trees are to be planted in a new forest in the North of England, which it is hoped will stretch eventually from coast to coast.

'The best time to plant a tree was twenty years ago. The second-best time is now.'

CHINESE PROVERB

PLANT A TREE

In the arboretum where I work, we plant on average sixty to seventy trees a year. In the UK, National Tree Week takes place in the last week of November each year to celebrate the winter tree-planting season, and anyone can take part.

1. To plant a tree of your own, simply push an individual seed or nut of a tree – be it an acorn, conker or hazelnut – about 2 centimetres deep in a pot of compost and cover it over with soil. (If planting a conker, check that it hasn't dried out by placing it in a container of water and discarding any seeds that float.)

2. Water it well and place the pot in a sheltered spot outdoors, where it will be protected from hard frosts and from animals such as mice and squirrels.

3. Keep watering it (but avoiding overwatering it) and repot it as the sapling grows.

4. Remember how big trees can grow and obtain permission from a landowner if necessary before planting your sapling.

When I work with groups, I like to encourage planting in areas such as village greens, school playing fields or on local farmland; however, there is always the invitation that if the tree grows too big and there isn't anywhere to replant it, it can be brought back and we will plant it in the arboretum.

TREES AS ECOSYSTEMS

Trees are much more than air-givers; they stabilise the ground beneath our feet and enable entire ecosystems to exist. Tree roots bind river banks and are therefore an essential part of our natural flood defences; they even help to create suitable habitats for fish such as salmon.[19] While tree roots are just as important as leaves in helping to provide the nutrients and water needed for a tree's growth and health, root systems not only benefit the individual tree, but help to keep the soil healthy by creating an environment where vital microorganisms can grow and flourish. These microscopic organisms are an integral part of ecosystems, playing critical roles in nutrient cycles, thereby regulating plant growth and soil structure.

It's recently been discovered that trees can communicate with each other using a complex underground network of fungi. They not only swap sugars, water and nutrients, but communicate warnings to one another about disease or pests, thereby helping to boost each other's immunity and nurture younger trees. Some communicate with other species besides their own, with deciduous trees communicating with evergreens and vice versa during their different growing seasons.

It's been found that 'hub trees', usually the older trees in the forest, act as mothers to seedlings, and that some are connected to hundreds of other trees, supporting them through their growth.[20]

'One touch of nature makes the whole world kin.'

**TROILUS AND CRESSIDA,
WILLIAM SHAKESPEARE,**

THE WORLD OF THE OAK

With an eye on ecosystems, let's take a closer look at the much-loved native *Quercus robur*, or English oak. Oak trees have been around much longer than humans and remnants of them have been discovered from the interglacial period around 300,000 years ago. This majestic tree has been respected throughout history for its durable timber. However, oak isn't just useful for its wood; it supports a wider variety of lifeforms than any other British tree. While its gnarly, furrowed bark houses hundreds of different types of insects, the stem and branches of its vast canopy are home to many different species of mammal and bird.

Insects such as bark lice – a tiny, beneficial insect that scavenges on dead bark, fungus and algae, which helps to clean the trunk of undesirables – are often found creating their protective webs on the oak. Mammals such as squirrels nest in the holes created over the years in old oaks, feasting on acorns (and I like to think they play their part in planting them, too, as I wonder just how many of the acorns that they bury actually get eaten). Birds such as the wonderful woodpecker will not only peck for insects living on these trees but will also nest in them. From these, right down to the other plants, fungus and lichens that share this fabulous habitat, the oak really does have a vital place in our environment.

'Might oaks from little acorns grow.'

PROVERB

OAK BEFORE ASH

If the oak is out before the ash
We shall surely have a splash;
If the ash is out before the oak
We shall surely have a soak.

I love this old wives' tale and it's one that our family stands by. We have an old ash tree to one side of our house, while on the other side there is an oak wood. Every year my son Elliot and I look out to see which of the mighty trees comes into leaf first. The proverb has not been wrong yet.

A SHORT HISTORY OF TREES

Until relatively recent times, our relationship with trees has primarily been one of worship, magic and respect. Perhaps early humans instinctively realised how important these incredible plants are to our mental and physical wellbeing. In some cultures, trees represent life itself, while others believe that humankind sprang from a tree. Trees and human life are profoundly linked, on many levels – from a sense of the sacred, to everyday survival.

HOLY TREES AND SACRED GROVES

The ancient Greeks believed that the first tree created by the gods was the oak, sacred to the king of the gods, Zeus, and that from it sprang the entire human race. The word *drŷs* means oak in Greek, and oak tree spirits were called dryads (although the name came to be associated with tree spirits generally). Based on this Greek term, the Roman historian Pliny the Elder conjectured in his *Natural History* that the Celtic word 'druid' had links with the oak, and indeed the druids also believed the oak to be the mightiest of trees, containing energy, power and strength. (In fact, the Old Irish word *dair* also means 'oak', a more likely source of the word.) To this day, many ancient forests have named druid oaks, such as those found at Salcey Forest in Northamptonshire and Burnham Beeches in Buckinghamshire.

According to Arthurian legend, the druid-like wizard Merlin worked his magic under a grove of oaks and his wand was said to be made from the topmost branch of an oak tree, while King Arthur's Round Table was said to be made of a long length of oak, as was the king's coffin. In addition to the oak, the ancient Britons believed aspen wood to be protective, so it was planted near houses and often used to make Celtic shields.

From the oak to the aspen and ash, to many other species, trees appear globally in mythology, religion and ancient traditions. The Vikings believed that an eternally green ash tree called Yggdrasil stood at the centre of the cosmos, spanning the nine worlds of Norse mythology, while in Buddhism, it is believed that the Buddha found enlightenment while sitting under the peepal or sacred fig tree. This same tree is sacred to Hindus, who revere it during religious festivals.

As well as being sacred in their own right, trees have traditionally played a part in many rituals. In Europe, couples were traditionally married under the branches of oaks long before the first churches were built.[21] Today, in Palestine, trees are planted for the birth of children: cedar for a boy and cypress for a girl; then, when the children grow up, branches from the trees are used to form the canopy for their wedding celebration. In the Côte d'Ivoire, Gold Coast bombax trees mark the spaces used by elders for political and judicial matters, while in Madagascar the baobab tree plays a similar role in denoting meeting places to discuss village matters.

Various forms of tree dressing also appear around the world. The Japanese decorate trees with white paper on which poems or wishes have been written, that are to be carried off on the breeze. In the Hindu festival of Raksha, coloured string is tied onto trees to call upon nature to protect families. Here, in the British Isles, it was an ancient practice to attach ribbons to 'clootie' trees growing at sacred sites such as holy wells or springs, as part of a healing ritual. Today, there is Tree Dressing Day, which we celebrate at the arboretum where I work by inviting the public to take a ribbon and tie it onto a designated tree, to make a wish and to say thank you to our great trees.[22]

We have a number of commemorative trees in the arboretum, as people often want to plant trees to celebrate births, friendships and to remember those who have passed away. In some countries, you can now have your ashes put into a biodegradable pod which is buried beneath a tree so that your remains essentially feed the tree as it grows: life going full circle.

It is perhaps no surprise that ancient people revered trees for their many different qualities, or that their reverence should be expressed in practical ways. An example of this is the ancient Ogham alphabet, which is centred on trees worshipped by the Celts. The alphabet is made up of a series of twenty characters, the markings consisting of a line or stem that is then crossed with slashes known as twigs. The first letter of the alphabet is the sound 'B' which is depicted by as a single straight line. The name of this character is Beith or Birch tree.

The Magical Birch, Lady of the Woods: the silver birch is known as the 'lady of the woods', a tree of enchantment and magic. An old Welsh custom was for a man to give the woman he loved a sprig of birch, and she would give one back if she felt the same way about him.

Birch bark has a paper-like texture and was used traditionally to write upon. I still have a little note in my desk written by a friend on a small piece of birch bark. The bark is also water resistant because it contains large amounts of resin, and in Lapland it is used to make cloaks and leggings to protect against the weather. Native North Americans also used the bark to line canoes.

Given the elegance of the tree, birch wood is surprisingly heavy and in the past was used to make bobbins, barrels and clogs. Toys were often made from the birch tree and the wood is still used in furniture-making throughout Europe.

The Mighty Oak: some believe that acorns were man's first food, and it is known from archaeological analysis of stone tools that flour was made out of acorns in prehistoric times.[23] The bark of the oak is often referred to as 'tanner's bark', as it is still used all over the world today for tanning leather. The bark would be stripped early in the spring and infused to create a purple dye used to colour wool.

Oak has been used over the centuries for shipbuilding. The Viking Ship Museum in Roskilde, Denmark houses the eleventh-century oak remains of magnificent longboats in which the Vikings sailed overseas on raiding expeditions; while around 5,500 oak trees were used to build the British warship HMS *Victory*, launched in 1765.

The official British Navy march, written in 1760 by David Garrick, is called 'Heart of the Oak' and goes:

Heart of oak are our ships,
Jolly tars are our men,
We always are ready;
Steady, boys, steady!
We'll fight and we'll conquer again and again.

The use of oak during the First World War resulted in a shortage of this majestic tree, which was the catalyst for the forming of the Forestry Commission in 1919.

Today, Nottinghamshire's Sherwood Forest remains home to Britain's most famous ancient tree, the Major Oak. It is said that the medieval outlaw Robin Hood held his meetings with his Merry Men within the hollow trunk of this veteran tree.

The Nurturing Beech: one of my favourite trees in the arboretum is a giant beech. Standing at over 33 metres in height, this impressive tree is believed to be around 200 years old. It's one of my favourite go-to spots; with its massive trunk, it sometimes feels like the tree is hugging me and not the other way around.

Beech trees are often referred to in history as the 'Mother of the Woods', associated with the qualities of protection and nurturing, which is perhaps why I feel such a sense of calm radiating from this kindly old tree. Another name for the tree is the Beech Queen, who stands proudly next to the Oak King.

In Europe, slivers of beech were used to write upon before paper was made, and the Anglo-Saxon word for beech was *boc*, which eventually became the word 'book'. Today, like the birch, the beech is often used to make furniture.

Beech nuts or 'mast' appear in the autumn and are edible – if bitter. Their oil content is high enough that pressed oil can be made from them. Young fresh beech leaves are a great addition to a salad, with a lovely sweet taste. They can also be steeped in vodka or gin with a quantity of sugar to produce an unusual liquor.

GET TO KNOW A TREE

With studies showing that many people don't even notice trees, why not take the time to find and focus on a tree near to you? It could be in your garden or at your workplace, a tree you remember from childhood or a tree that you pass daily.

Notice it change through the different seasons.
How does this tree make you feel?
Perhaps take the time to draw it or photograph it below.
Take a picnic near it or simply lean against the trunk and breathe.

FROM SACRED GROVES
TO MODERN FEARS

So how has our relationship with trees changed over the ages? It seems to me that people today have almost been taught to fear the woods, even though we no longer have any real reason to do so. The saying 'out of the woods' means that you are over the worst or clear of danger, and originates with the Romans in an era when European forests were vast and getting lost in the woods represented a real danger. Many traditional nursery rhymes or children's stories often have a baddie, be it a wicked witch or a hungry wolf, who can be found lurking in the woods. In modern horror films such as *The Blair Witch Project*, *The Cabin in the Woods* and *The Forest*, woods and forests are depicted as dark places surrounded with magic and mystery, where a curious cabin sitting in the heart of the woods is still to be approached with caution...

My family and I actually live in the woods. Our home is a quaint cottage that overlooks parkland and fields but which is nestled in ancient woodland. Somewhat ironically, the forest is at its darkest in the height of summer when the trees' great canopies are lush and full. This is when we wander in the woods for our daily dog walk, maybe with relief after a tough day or perhaps enlivened by one of my children's many imaginative adventures. I feel incredibly lucky to be surrounded by such awe-inspiring nature, with its ever-giving health-enhancing qualities. Yet a question I am often asked is: 'Aren't you scared?' This always floors me. Why would I be scared – and of what? The peaceful wildlife with which I'm lucky to share my garden with, the gentle sway and comforting sounds of the trees in the breeze? Even in the harshest of winters, this woodland is my sanctuary.

I put my own good health down to the trees around me. My recent recovery from serious physical illness, although at times long and difficult, could be seen as something of a miracle; and I sometimes wonder just how different it would have been for me if I lived in a town or a city and didn't have nature's first aid chest so readily available on my doorstep.

TREE MEDICINE

Many trees have been, and still are, used in medicine. The key ingredient of aspirin, one of the first drugs ever to come into production, is salicylic acid, which functions as a plant hormone and is found most notably in the bark of the willow tree, or Salix. I have drunk willow bark tea that I made on a wild food and medicine course run by an experienced herbalist – and it has to be the bitterest thing I have ever tasted in my life!

Over the centuries, our diets (and probably our palates) have changed incredibly, from being quite bitter to quite sweet, with sugar or artificial sweeteners being added to many manufactured foodstuffs – so it's no wonder there has been a rise in digestive health issues. People regularly used to take bitter tinctures and elixirs for healthy living and healthy digestion. The phrase 'a bitter pill' comes from the health benefits offered by the many bitter medicines that were once widely used and made from the plants around us.

Today, there are some excellent courses available if you do wish to make your own tinctures, or you can easily obtain ready-made plant supplements from health food shops. Whenever using naturally sourced ingredients, do take professional advice. Also remember to respect the health of the tree in addition to looking after your own wellbeing.

For instance, when collecting bark from a tree, it's preferable only to take the bark in spring, as this gives the tree a chance to recover. Care must be taken not to remove the rings of the bark, known as girdling the tree, as girdling will prevent the tree from obtaining the food and water it needs to survive and will eventually kill it. It's therefore best to use bark removed from a small branch that has been sawn off just beyond the branch collar. This allows the tree to heal itself naturally.

Ash: this tree was thought to have healing properties and a spoonful of sap from the tree was often given to newborn babies, while sick children would be passed through the branches of a seedling ash in the hope it would cure them.

Beech: the leaves are cooling and healing, and make a soothing poultice if applied to skin conditions.

Cedar of Lebanon: native to the Mediterranean and Asia, this tree's fragrant resin was used for embalming by the ancient Egyptians and to get rid of parasites. Today, the oil is used by aromatherapists to soothe anxiety and treat skin and respiratory conditions. The smell of cedar wood is striking and very appealing. We recently lost a large cedar to honey fungus in the arboretum and when the tree was taken down you could still smell the scent of cedar for weeks afterwards in the wood.

Ginkgo (also known as maidenhair): native to China, this tree has been found to have high antioxidant and anti-inflammatory properties. I once met a spritely elderly man who swore by eating a young ginkgo leaf a day for his joints. It is also known to improve brain efficiency and activity.

GINKGO TEA FOR A HEALTHY BRAIN

Ginkgo makes an excellent tea with health benefits. However, it is not recommended to drink this tea if you're on any other medication, or are pregnant or breastfeeding.

2 teaspoons dried/5 fresh ginkgo leaves (best picked in late summer) per serving

1 drinking cup of freshly boiled water

1. Add the ginkgo leaves to the cup of freshly boiled water and steep for 10 minutes.

2. Strain and drink immediately, once or twice a day.

Oak: this tree's bark was traditionally used to create a tonic that was useful, if gargled, for healing sore throats, as it has antiseptic properties. Oak bark was also used for the treatment of diarrhoea and, if mixed with acorns, provided an antidote to poisoning. The leaves, if bruised, can be used externally on wounds to help ease inflammation. The acorns can be used to make a bitter-tasting, caffeine-free coffee, which contains nutritive properties and aids poor digestion and colic.

Pine: this tree's oil is beneficial for the respiratory system.

Silver birch: the bark is a diuretic and antiseptic, and contains pain-relieving properties. Easily made into a tea, it also lowers cholesterol. The young leaves can be used as a diuretic and made into a cleansing tea.

Willow: white willow and black willow are most commonly used for their medicinal properties. As a herbal supplement, willow can be taken in the form of tea, a tincture, or even by chewing the bark – however, this last isn't recommended as you can't be sure how much salicin (the source of salicylic acid) you might consume.

Yew: a more recent medicinal find comes from the yew tree, or Taxus. This tree, although highly poisonous, has been found to contain chemicals known as taxanes, which is said to help prevent new cancer cells forming. Smouldering wet foliage from the yew can also be used to create an insecticidal smoke that repels most biting insects.

WILLOW ARTISTS' CHARCOAL

Willow can be used to make artists' charcoal, art being good for the soul and a form of practical therapy. Whenever I've made charcoal, these little sticks of burnt wood end up being used by the whole family to create crazy, messy works of art until we can no longer hold the tiny black stubs in our fingers and they disappear into nothing.

It's easy to make your own drawing charcoal:

1. Cut small lengths of thin willow and strip off the bark. Allow them to dry overnight.

2. Place the willow sticks in a heatproof sealable tin (such as an old metal biscuit tin). Once you've filled your tin and sealed it, place it carefully into a fire. This could be the glowing embers of a wood burner or an outdoor camp fire.

3. Leave the tin in the fire's embers overnight and remove in the morning. Be aware that if you want to check your sticks while they are in the fire, the tin will need an hour to cool down before you open it.

4. Remove the lid – and discover your sticks of artists' charcoal.

BACH FLOWER REMEDIES

Bach Flower Remedies were first prepared in the 1930s by Dr Edward Bach, and are tinctures made from various plants, including trees, to address health-influencing emotional states. Rescue Remedy is probably the most famous of these, used for comfort during difficult times. It is a blend of five active ingredients, one of which is taken from the cherry plum tree, which helps to keep a balanced mind.

I used Rescue Remedy many years ago to help steady my nerves when I took my driving test, and was so calm that I passed first time. Used sparingly, it's great for pets too. I give it to my dog, Dotty, to help soothe her when she's scared by fireworks.

Oak is no stranger among the Bach Remedies either and is used to treat despair, as well as to treat those suffering from a nervous breakdown; it's said to be a calming yet energising remedy. My favourite, the beech tree, is used to treat intolerance and irritability, and to encourage understanding.

FOREST BATHING

I am a huge fan of the many health benefits
that come from simply hanging around among
the trees. These benefits have given rise to the
Japanese-led practice of *shinrin-yoku* or 'forest
bathing'. You would be forgiven if you thought you
might need a towel and your swimwear, which is what
I'm usually asked when introducing this practice to people
in the sessions I lead. You don't! It's simply the art of immersing
yourself in a wooded environment to gain huge health benefits not
only physically but mentally and emotionally, too.

When I first came across forest bathing a few years ago, I searched
for more information about it, and the more I read, the more I
realised that this was something I'd actually been doing for years in
the course of my daily life. I knew all too well the relief I felt when
I was among the trees – but it was great to have some science to
explain it.

The Japanese started studying the benefits of forest bathing scientifically forty years ago and found that trees release essential oils
called phytoncides. The trees use these fabulous oils to help defend
themselves from pests and diseases, and it's been discovered that we
humans benefit from them too. As we wander around a woodland
or forest, we inhale the oils, which have a direct effect on our nervous system.

The discoveries are astounding: within as little as fifteen minutes of being in a wooded environment, our heart rate will be reduced, our blood pressure will fall and our cortisol levels are balanced, thereby promoting stress relief. People suffering from pain have reported a lessening of their symptoms and it has been found that those recovering from illness and injury will recover much more quickly and effectively than those who are not exposed to phytoncides. People who struggle with sleep disorders show improved sleep patterns after forest bathing, while those struggling with mental health and mood disorders such as anxiety, depression and PTSD have reported great relief and recovery. In addition, it is thought the body's anti-cancer cells have been found to flourish after forest bathing. Our immune systems are greatly enhanced by the seemingly simple act of going for a walk in the woods, and the knock-on effect of regular 'bathing' is overall wellbeing and life enhancement.

The recommended dose of forest bathing is two hours a week for life-changing effects. I tell people that if you don't have two hours a week to spare, even fifteen minutes can be important. The effects will stay with you for at least a week, sometimes even longer. With many different cultures now practising forest bathing, some businesses insisting their employees forest bathe, and certain doctors prescribing it for their patients, perhaps those deep dark woodlands don't seem so scary after all!

When people say, 'I walk my dogs through the woods every day – what's the difference between that and forest bathing?' I always reply by asking where their minds are. You see, life is so chaotic that our restless minds are constantly filled with thoughts. Some people aren't even aware of the dog they are walking, let alone where they are and how their body feels.

This is why I like to teach people simple mindfulness techniques to enhance their experience of this wonderful practice. I teach them to slow right down, to take the time to reconnect not only with their surroundings but with themselves. Nearly everyone I work with says they feel like they need permission to do this for themselves. Yet when we become mindful, or fully present, we open up all of our senses. We suddenly notice the little things, the things that are always there but which we are usually so disconnected from – whether it be the way raindrops form on leaves or the sound the wind makes through different trees, the feel of tree bark and how it makes our hands tingle, the smell of leaf litter and its crunch under our feet.

A woodland has a great ability to bring you back to yourself, something that I have often experienced for myself. I remember a particularly difficult day when I found myself sitting under a great pine tree. My plan was to take a few moments to reconnect with myself and find some calm. However, my mind carried on ruminating over the day but I didn't even realise I was doing this, until the tree brought me back to the present moment. The wind was blowing quite strongly and all of a sudden I could feel the tree moving; the gentle sway of the whole tree in the wind was calming and hypnotic, yet incredibly grounding. The sensation of being gently rocked by this great tree was wonderful and the perfect reminder to live in the now, in harmony with the elements.

FOREST BATHE YOURSELF CALM

Take a forest bath in your nearest woodland.

Forest bathing is not about taking a hike; you don't need to
walk for miles and miles. Slow the pace right down.

**Practise mindfulness techniques as you move through the wood
by opening up your senses: what can you hear, what can you
see, what does it smell like and how do you feel?**

Breathe.

HOW DO YOU FEEL ABOUT TREES?

· ·

· ·

WHAT ARE YOUR THOUGHTS AFTER GETTING TO KNOW A TREE?
HOW DO THESE CHANGE WITH THE SEASONS?

· ·

· ·

WHAT ARE YOUR THOUGHTS AND FEELINGS
AFTER A FOREST-BATHING SESSION?

· ·

· ·

Seasons & Weather

3

I've always wondered which comes first: the weather or the season? Which determines which? I think nature decides, which is what I tell people whenever I hear phrases such as 'spring is early' or 'autumn's late'.

What we think the weather and the seasons should be doing and what they are actually doing are usually two very different things. The calendar may tell us when each season should start and finish, but more often than not the seasons merge and change according to their own rhythms.

THE SEASONS

In my job, I take a great deal of notice of the seasonal changes and the weather. Autumn is always a million-dollar question in the arboretum: is it going to be early or late? Will it be a good one? What will the colours look like? For me, autumn is here when I can smell it – that mushroomy crispness in the air, those curious mists that start to appear in the morning. I glimpse the subtle changes of colour in the trees, and the animals start to alter their behaviours. At the other end of the year, spring arrives for me when I first spot the tiny green buds appearing and developing on plants just before they burst into life; the grass looks a little greener and the animals begin to go about their spring activities. It is when I notice the birds begin to sing a little more loudly in the morning and migrant birds start to appear. I may spot a bumblebee looking for those vital early flowers and, where we live, frogs begin to appear in their hundreds.

THE SEASONS AND OUR PLANET

Our seasons and their weather are caused by the Earth's tilt on its axis. Summer takes place in the hemisphere of the Earth that is tilted towards the Sun, while winter happens in the hemisphere tilted away from the Sun.

It's generally thought that the Earth's tilt was caused during the creation of the solar system itself, when the collision of matter and other planets placed Earth in the position it occupies today. Happily, the tilt of our planet creates the perfect conditions for generating the weather systems that allow life to exist; if this tilt hadn't happened or our planet occupied a slightly different position in the solar system, one side of the Earth would be too hot and the other side too cold, and life would not be able to thrive as it does or even exist at all.

The Moon also has a small but important part to play in this system. Its gravitational pull creates slight, small changes in the Earth's tilt without which the seasonal changes would be much greater. In fact, the relationship between the Moon and the seasons is reflected in the names given to the Moon's phases by various cultures around the world. Some North American indigenous peoples call February's Full Moon the 'Snow Moon' or 'Hunger Moon' owing to the cold, snowy weather that often occurs this month, while November's Full Moon is known as the 'Frost Moon', because winter frosts usually begin then. Many early Native Americans used the phases of the Moon to keep track of the seasons, with some tribes having four seasons while others recognised five.

FIVE SEASONS

Like some Native American tribes, Chinese culture recognises five seasons. These are spring, summer and late summer, autumn and winter. Each season is associated with an elemental energy:

SPRING AND THE ELEMENT OF WOOD

The beginning of the seasonal cycle, a time of birth and new beginnings. Like the spreading branches of a tree, spring provides structure and thrusts forward. This season is about moving forward and future vision.

SUMMER AND THE ELEMENT OF FIRE

An active time of warmth and growth, when nature is moving. Fire is about relationships; at this time of year, we feel sociable, warm and uplifted.

LATE SUMMER AND THE ELEMENT OF EARTH

This is the extra, shortest Chinese season, which only lasts a few weeks. This is a time of abundance, nourishment and stability. Earth gives us its harvest and nourishes us with its food.

AUTUMN AND THE ELEMENT OF METAL

A time when nature lets go of what is not needed. It then recycles itself to ensure the next cycle has what it needs to aid growth. Metal helps us to understand that we are connected to everything.

WINTER AND THE ELEMENT OF WATER

This is a time of rest, when nature hibernates and incubates its energy supplies, ready for the coming cycles. Water is about our ability to flow, and about how we can relate our energy to the many different forms that water presents in nature.

SEASONS AROUND THE WORLD

While most parts of the world experience four seasons, there are other parts of the Earth where the seasonal change differs. The tropics, for instance, only experience two seasons: wet and dry. Again, this is caused by the Earth's tilt, which means the tropics have more exposure to sunlight than the rest of the planet.

Areas nearer the Indian Ocean experience three seasons: winter, summer and monsoon. Bangladesh, which sits in this part of the world, divides these three main seasons into six according to cultural traditions and agricultural practices. The Bengali year is divided into the following periods:

GRISHMA

It begins with summer when the weather is hot and dry with the occasional storm

BARSA

Monsoon season spreads from June to August and brings 85 per cent of the yearly rainfall

SHARAT

Autumn is between August and October and brings about a temperature decrease and change in humidity

HEMANTA

October to December
brings late autumn and an
even bigger decrease
in temperature

SHIT

Winter is between
December and February
and brings with it the most
pleasant temperatures
ranging between
11°C and 20°C

BASANTA

The final season is
spring, when the weather
warms up, there is a
breeze in the air and the
occasional storm.[24]

CELEBRATING THE SEASONS

Cultures all over the world celebrate the changing seasons with rituals and festivals. These tend to take place on set calendar days and mark varying periods of change, growth and abundance. They also mark significant events such as the equinoxes and solstices.

At the spring and autumn equinoxes, the Sun shines directly on the Equator and the length of day and night is roughly equal. In the Northern Hemisphere, the spring equinox takes place in the month of March, whereas in the Southern Hemisphere (Australia, South America and southern Africa), it occurs in September.

The summer solstice occurs each year when the Earth's tilt means that the Sun is at its highest position in the sky relative to the horizon, while the winter solstice takes place when the Earth's tilt means the Sun's arc across the sky is at its lowest, relative to the horizon. The seasons experienced by the Northern and Southern Hemispheres differ by six months, so that when it is winter in the Northern Hemisphere, it is summer in the Southern Hemisphere.

SPRING CELEBRATIONS

Spring is traditionally a great cause for celebration and a time to mark the beginning of new life. For many cultures, it is also a time of returning warmth after long cold months, when crops can be sown, food sources renewed and the beauty of life is celebrated. The Japanese Sakura or Cherry Blossom Festival, is a wonderful example of this, when friends and families wander, picnic and party beneath flowering cherry trees.

Besides celebrating regeneration, spring is traditionally a time for refreshing what we have – which can include a good old spring clean. The festival of new life or Nowruz, also known as the Persian New Year, falls on the spring equinox and is celebrated across Western Asia, Central Asia and the Black Sea Basin. During this time, people celebrate by cleaning and painting houses and hanging flowers on doors and windows.

The Hindu festival of Holi is also celebrated during the spring equinox. This ancient religious festival is a colourful affair where communities come together to sing and dance and throw coloured powder over one another. It is a celebration of the victory of good over evil and the start of spring after winter.

Similarly, Ostara used to be celebrated by Europeans to mark the arrival of spring, and is still celebrated by some modern pagans today. It is the origin of the Christian festival of Easter. Ostara was a Germanic goddess of spring and dawn, who had a rabbit by her side as a companion and carried magical eggs that regenerated life. Many people today decorate eggs and eat chocolate eggs to mark the arrival of spring at Easter.

The ancient Celts celebrated Beltane, known today as May Day, to mark the arrival of summer. For the Celts, this day represented the halfway point in the year when magic could be found. Great bonfires were lit during this time and people would dance around a May pole tied with coloured ribbons to bring energy to the coming summer months, a practice that still continues in some areas.

In times gone by, Swedish women and girls would similarly bathe in a river in the summer in the belief that by doing so they would encourage rain for the crops; and at midsummer, Swedish villagers would dance around decorated poles called *midsommarstång* to celebrate the summer solstice, the longest day of the year.

In Poland, people celebrate the midsummer festival of Wianki, whose roots lie in an ancient pagan fertility festival. As part of these festivities, young women create wonderful floral garlands and throw them into the river, where young men in boats do their best to catch their girlfriend's wreath.

The autumn equinox takes place in September in the Northern Hemisphere, and March in the Southern Hemisphere. Autumn is traditionally the time of year for harvest festivals and celebrating nature's bounty.

Chinese culture marks the end of summer with the Moon Festival, which is held when the Moon is at its brightest. As part of the festivities, people light lanterns and take walks in the moonlight. They also eat moon cakes, traditional little cakes that are shared between family and friends, and which have a baked egg yolk in the centre of the cake to resemble the Moon.

Prayers of gratitude have been offered, and special thanksgiving festivals have been celebrated as far back as the ancient Greeks, who would fill a goat's horn with fruit and grains to give thanks for the harvest. In North America, the pilgrims celebrated their first Thanksgiving in 1621 after a hard first winter. With the help of Native Americans who showed them how to hunt and what plants they could eat, they managed to survive and celebrated their first harvest with a feast of turkey, cranberries, sweet potatoes and pumpkins.

In the Celtic wheel of the year, Mabon is an autumn festival when communities come together to give thanks for the year's harvest and hospitality is in the air. It is also a traditional time of year to visit the graves of loved ones and honour the dead by leaving an offering of an apple or another natural item; in fact, it is said to be bad luck if you pass a graveyard during this time and do not leave something.

Ancient Romans celebrated winter by honouring the god of agriculture and time, Saturn, at a festival called the Saturnalia, held from 17 and 23 December, which is a predecessor of our modern celebration of Christmas. Homes were decorated with evergreen branches and lamps were lit to ward off the dark.

On the longest night of the year at the winter solstice, Iranians celebrate the victory of the Sun god over the darkness in the festival of Shab-e Yalda, which translates as 'night of birth'. Communities come together to light up the dark with fires, to feast and make wishes for the coming year.

The Chinese celebrate winter solstice with a celebration called Dongzhi, which means 'winter arrives', on which they welcome the arrival of longer days and the energy of the new year ahead. It's believed by many that this is the day when everyone becomes one year older.

Scandinavians celebrate Jul, and traditions include decorating a Christmas tree and a yule log. The yule log was originally a full-sized log set in a long barn, decorated and set to smoulder for twelve days to add energy to the growing Sun. The decorated tree was usually an evergreen tree that was brought inside and decorated with candles, nuts and berries to symbolise light and life.

CREATE YOUR OWN SEASONAL DISPLAY

Many people like to bring the seasons into their living space, be it in the form of a bunch of daffodils arranged in a vase or an evergreen swag draped over the mantelpiece. I like to place a vase of seasonal flowers as the centrepiece on the table. However, I also display other things alongside the flowers, depending on the time of year. In spring, for instance, I put out an old, abandoned, found bird's nest, while conkers, pumpkins and pine cones are part of the autumn decorations.

Why not make your own seasonal display? Mix cultivated flowers with wildflowers (including what many may call weeds) from the hedgerows – though be careful not to pick endangered plants or to uproot the whole plant. Add twigs, cones, evergreen foliage and other seasonal items to your display to symbolise the different seasons. With a bit of imagination, you can create a fantastic seasonal celebration of nature.

HOW THE SEASONS
AFFECT US

The seasons physically and emotionally affect us humans, but as we are linked to nature after all, it's not really a surprise. Science has found that our brain patterns actually change with the seasons, affecting our mood, our immunity and changing the parts of the brain we access to carry out cognitive tasks.[25] Similar to the animals around us, we react and adapt to the changes surrounding us in nature, even if we don't notice that we're doing so.

A Belgian study carried out on people's brain function over the four seasons had particularly interesting results: the participants were cut off from all seasonal clues and asked to carry out a range of tasks. While the results of the tasks didn't differ over the four seasons, the way in which the participants used their brains did. The studies found that during an attention task the subject's brain function peaked during the summer months whereas there was much less brain function in the winter months for the same task. For memory tasks, it was found that brain activity peaked in the autumn and was at its lowest in the spring. The study also found that our metabolism changes with the seasons so we are more likely to gain weight in the winter, and that we see colour differently in the summer to the rest of the year.[26]

We associate different colours with different seasons: greens and yellows may come with spring and summer, perhaps deep earthy tones like orange come with autumn and we may associate winter with the colour white or red. But science tells us that we actually see the colours differently, too. This fascinating study found that our visual systems changed and responded to seasonal changes. When asked to view different colours throughout the year, with test conditions staying identical, the study found that people's visual perception changed with the seasons and there were marked differences on what people thought true yellow was, for example.

Interestingly, our genes also behave differently according to the season, which has an effect on our immune system – with some genes being more active in the winter months and some more active in the summer months. The findings of the research show we are more susceptible to certain diseases like autoimmune disorders and cardiovascular disease over certain seasons.[27]

HIBERNATING HUMANS

Over the years, I've given a great deal of thought to the subject of hibernation and wonder if this is something that humans once did. Maybe this is the reason why our brains behave differently during the winter months?

Hibernation is all about conserving energy; it's a state of inactivity that allows the body to store and preserve energy supplies while eating very little. However, it's not about going to sleep for months on end, as some may think. Our human bodies are not actually designed to hibernate as an animal does: a small animal can keep its heart pumping at a body temperature of 1°C, whereas the human heart could stop if the body temperature were to drop to 25°C.[28]

The dormouse famously hibernates each winter by rolling into a tight little ball in a nest on the ground. Its body temperature and heart rate are lowered and its breathing slows. In hibernation, the rodent shuts its body down to the extent that it becomes rigid and cold to the touch. The dormouse can stay in hibernation for up to six months before it rouses from its deep sleep in warmer weather.

At the other end of the scale, black bears can hibernate for up to eight months without food and water, during which time they remain safely tucked up in their den, having gained as many calories and energy reserves as they can during autumn. Some bears wake up for short periods during hibernation, when they venture out of the den for short periods whereas some simply stir inside their dens.

Some species of insects hibernate. Bumblebees usually sleep through winter: newly mated queens will burrow into soft ground or find a log or rock under which to shelter, then emerge at the start of spring to lay eggs. Some bumblebees can wake up confused on warmer winter days, and recent seasonal changes have seen a marked alteration in bumblebee hibernation behaviour with some queens starting nests in warmer winters instead of hibernating.

There is also a species of fish that goes into a type of hibernation: the arctic cod can put itself into a state of dormancy by lowering its metabolism, and its blood contains a sort of antifreeze.

It's thought that early humans evolved in the tropics, where there would have been a consistent food supply and conditions weren't harsh enough to require a survival skill such as hibernation. Yet it seems that early humankind did practise a type of hibernation during the colder months in the Ice Age, by spending up to twenty-three hours per day in their cave – not surprising given their lack of warm clothing in which to go out and brave the elements.

However, even in the 1800s families would get together and sleep for up to sixteen hours a day during the winter. In the 1900s, a starving community in Russia was found to carry out a type of hibernation called 'lotska', during which they would head indoors at the first sign of snow, gather around their stove and fall into a deep sleep or 'lotska'. They would then wake up once a day to consume some bread and water and wouldn't come out of this state until spring arrived.[29]

While no evidence has been found of this type of behaviour in modern times, if you look at the way we live in the West, I suppose we do carry out a type of hibernation during the winter months. We hunker down for cosy nights in; we gather together with our friends and family; we may feel more tired and lacking in energy than at other times of the year; we wrap ourselves up warm; and the idea of an early night tucked up in bed with a warm cup of herbal tea is much more attractive than in the summer months, when we can enjoy long evenings outside if the weather allows.

'Long sleeps the summer in the seed.'

**IN MEMORIAM,
ALFRED TENNYSON**

SEASONAL AFFECTIVE DISORDER

Seasonal affective disorder (SAD) is a type of depression that is related to the changes in the seasons. It usually starts in the autumn and continues into the winter months. SAD is more common in countries that are further north of the Equator, such as in Scandinavia, where there are greater changes between weather patterns and light levels at different times of the year. While the exact causes are still unclear, it is thought that a number of factors can contribute to making us feel down in this way.

Light levels in particular have a major part to play, and as winter deepens, this has an effect on our brains.[30] When light hits the back of our eye, messages are sent to the parts of our brain that affect sleep, appetite, activity and mood, with some people needing more light than others and being more likely to be affected by SAD.

As a SAD sufferer myself, I am greatly affected by light levels; some may think that as I spend more time outdoors than the average person this wouldn't be the case, but it still is. To help myself, I use light therapy as well as spending as much time in natural daylight as I possibly can. If I am indoors I will try to sit near a window, I practise mindfulness and exercise, and I use an alarm clock that mimics the effect of sunlight. Half an hour before the alarm is due to sound, a light comes on, dimly at first, then brighter, as if to mimic the rising Sun, which means that I always wake before the alarm rings and usually feel refreshed. My light-giving alarm also mimics a sunset at bedtime; again, I set the light to work for half an hour and it gradually fades into darkness as I fall asleep.

These lights and others like them have been found to be very effective for people suffering not just from SAD but depression in general, as well as sleep disorders and other conditions. Some people use light boxes, which are medically certified to treat SAD with a brightness of over 2,500 lux. The positioning of the light is important as the light needs to fall on both the eyes, and many people will spend several minutes a day in front of their SAD lamp to alleviate symptoms.

TOO MUCH SUN

SAD doesn't just strike because of lack of light; at the other extreme, too much light can affect us as well, with some people feeling as wired by excessive light as by drinking too much caffeine. Too much sunlight can actually turn off melatonin production, the hormone that is responsible for our circadian (our sleeping and waking) cycles.

We need darkness as well as light; it's vital for getting proper rest and it's calming for us. The dark stimulates melatonin production, which sends a signal to our brains telling our bodies that it's time to rest. However, light exposure at the wrong times can interfere with this cycle and in a world where we use so much artificial light, a good night's sleep can be hard to come by.

For a better night's sleep, try to limit screen time by switching off electronic devices at least two hours before bedtime. If you go to bed at a regular time, set a timer to remind yourself, and then use those gadget-free hours to wind down, spend quality time with loved ones, play board games, walk, do simple art projects or read. Avoid taking your phone into your bedroom or switch the notifications off if you have to. Do this at least for a week and keep a diary of how you feel during this time to gauge the improvements in your sleep.

INTO THE LIGHT

We can take daylight for granted, but some countries see no daylight for months on end during the winter months. Antarctica has only two seasons: six months of daylight in the summer and six months of darkness in the winter. During the summer, Antarctica is on the side of the Earth that faces the Sun, while during the six long months of darkness it is on the side that faces away from the Sun. Antarctica is the coldest place on our planet and the only plants that can survive there are lichens, mosses and algae. It is considered a desert as it receives very little rain and snow, and it is made up of thick sheets of ice that are thousands of years old.

Utqiagvik, formerly known as Barrow, is a city located high up in Alaska in North America. It is one of the most northern communities in the world and has been home to the indigenous Inuit people for over a thousand years. Like Antarctica, Utqiagvik has a desert climate with very little rain and is very cold. Here the Sun sets on 18 November and stays below the horizon for about sixty-six days. When the Sun fully rises in May, the population is then bathed in daylight for three months.

Norway is similarly known as the land of the midnight Sun, as the most northerly parts of the country can experience sunlight more or less around the clock between May and July. However, in the south of Norway, the picturesque town of Rjukan has its specific location to thank for its lack of winter sunlight, as the mountains that hug this little town block out the sunlight for six months of the year between September and March. In 2013, the town installed giant rotating mirrors powered by wind and solar energy to reflect the Sun onto the town's market square, meaning that at least in one area you can bathe in the warmth of the much-needed sunlight.

'Be like a tree and let the dead leaves drop.'

RUMI, SUFI POET

SEASONS WITHIN OURSELVES

While working with people at the arboretum, I often refer to the seasons for inspiration. I encourage visitors to look at what nature is doing and how we can relate the season to ourselves and our lives.

Why not take a moment now to reflect on how each season makes you feel and relates to your own life?

Here are some suggestions to get you started:

SPRING: traditionally thought of as the start of the seasonal cycle and a time of new life, when nature wakes up refreshed and energised. Spring encourages us to look at new beginnings, to refresh and energise ourselves, encouraging our personal growth.

SUMMER: everything in nature is flourishing, growing and lush. The nights are lighter and the temperature is warmer. Summer encourages us to be brighter, happier and sunnier and to find gratitude for the world around us.

AUTUMN: nature is changing with ease and grace. This is when deciduous trees let go of their leaves and transform. This is something we can all take inspiration from, be it a change in behaviours, thought-patterns or habits – the letting go of things we hold on to that are unhelpful to us and the transformation that comes with this wonderful process.

WINTER: now nature is recharging, dormant and resting. We all need time to rest and digest to regenerate and carry out self-care to be the best version of ourselves. From this follows a calm and peaceful you.

Take a moment to jot your findings and reflections in your notebook. Perhaps you could turn them into a meditation, song lyrics or poem?

WEATHER

The UK has a temperate climate, which means we generally have wet, cool winters and wet, warm summers. We rarely encounter extremes of weather in the way that other countries do, although the weather around the UK can vary geographically – ranging from drier, warmer summers and milder winters in the south of the country, to wet, cool summers and harsher winters in the north. However, throughout the UK and Europe, the weather system is very influenced by the jet stream and the Gulf Stream.

THE JET STREAM

This consists of a core of strong winds blowing from east to west about five to seven miles above the Earth's surface. Sitting high up in the troposphere, the jet stream flows between two layers of the atmosphere that have very different temperatures. The greater the difference in temperature, the faster this stream of air flows, often moving at speeds exceeding 100 mph. The jet stream moves whole weather systems, and its position and strength are therefore used by meteorologists for forecasting.

Pollutants and greenhouse gases have been found to play a huge part in shaping the jet stream's behaviour, with there being a marked change in the jet stream's pattern over the past fifteen years. As climate change affects the flow of the jet stream, we are more likely to experience floods, summer droughts and wildfires in the future.[31] In the summer of 2018, this was evident when the jet stream demonstrated a wavy pattern known as quasi-resonant amplification, which had costly weather effects in the shape of scorching temperatures and wildfires in western USA, flooding in eastern USA and drought and heat over Europe.

THE GULF STREAM

This is the strongest and most important ocean current in the world. Driven by wind and water, the Gulf Stream moves warm water from the Caribbean Sea into the Atlantic Ocean, then on towards the British Isles. This vast ocean current ensures the UK's relatively mild winters and temperate summers.

However, climate change and the melting of the ice caps are having a detrimental impact on the Gulf Stream, slowing it down. This has an impact on our weather but rather than heat things up, it can actually cool things down.[32]

CLIMATE CHANGE

Some years, it can feel like there are no significant seasonal changes. It can seem pretty grim all year round, even though the winter may not be especially wintery, just cold and damp with no great frosts or snowfall to excite us. I've noticed more and more how the seasons seem different to those I remember from my childhood. Why is this so? Climate change perhaps? I think so.

Situated in the middle of the hugely powerful jet and Gulf Streams, it seems that, like the rest of the planet, the UK cannot escape the effects of climate change – and in fact we are already seeing them. Climate change is a lasting change in long-term weather patterns which occurs over a period of time. Since the 1950s there has been a steep climb in global temperatures linked to climate change.

There are two causes of climate change. One type is naturally occurring such as those, for example, caused by El Niño and La Niña. These are the names of the opposite phases of what is known as the El Niño-Southern Oscillation (ENSO) cycle. These complex weather patterns occur every few years and involve the natural change of temperature in pools of water in the Equatorial Pacific Ocean. The effects of these temperature changes are seen in rainfall over lands which then suffer from either flooding or drought.[33]

The other reason for climate change is human activity. From burning fossil fuels, deforestation, traffic pollution, creating rubbish dumps, releasing CFCs into the atmosphere, and using nuclear power and chemicals, we seem to be doing a good job of leaving a dirty big footprint on our planet.[34] Yet it seems that still, for a lot of people, it's all too easy to ignore its effects until it comes knocking on the door. The simple fact is that it is already knocking on our front door: we are already seeing a rise in heavier localised rainfall that causes devastating flooding, and with the UK being an island, we are one of the most vulnerable countries in Europe to coastal flooding.

In the UK, the average yearly rainfall is around 885 millimetres but the impact of climate change means that we are now often seeing not enough rain as well too much rain. In addition to increased localised flooding, droughts are fast having more impact than just the occasional hosepipe ban in the summer. We have had a taste of things warming up, with the highest ever temperature of 38.7°C recorded in July 2019 when the UK sizzled in the hottest summer on record.

Heat stress is linked to these hotter temperatures, with people becoming ill as the body is unable to cool itself, and sadly more vulnerable people die. Our natural fauna and flora are changing too: flowers may bloom earlier in response to warmer temperatures earlier in the year, while pollinating insects are becoming scarcer, birds migrate earlier and animals leave hibernation earlier too – and the knock-on effect of all of this could be changes in entire ecosystems. This will all have an effect on human life.[35]

TAKE A STAND AGAINST CLIMATE CHANGE

We can all do something to help tackle climate change.
No matter how big or small, changes in our own lives can
go a long way to help our planet.

Here are some simple steps to consider:

GET INFORMED – educate yourself and others
about climate change, and spread the word.

USE ENERGY WISELY – turn lights off, unplug TVs and computers
when not in use, wash in cold or warm water rather than
hot, buy goods that have a high energy efficiency rating.

TAKE A LOOK AT YOUR DIET – don't waste food, eat vegetarian
a few times a week and have a go at growing your own veg.
This type of sustainable diet encourages minimal environmental
impact, as the livestock industry alone is responsible for
around 18 per cent of greenhouse gas emissions.

TRAVEL WITH CARE – walk, car-share or
use public transport, and fly less.

RECYCLE, RECYCLE, RECYCLE

**JOIN A CAMPAIGN OR ORGANISATION TO SHOW YOUR
SUPPORT IN THE FIGHT AGAINST CLIMATE CHANGE**

PREDICTING WEATHER THE NATURAL WAY

Working outdoors on a daily basis, I experience all weathers, so you might think that I would consult the weather forecast daily, not only to plan my day but to figure out what clothes to wear. The truth is I seldom look at the weather forecast; instead, I have learnt over the years to pack everything, just in case. I layer up and layer down according to the temperature and I always have a raincoat and a sunhat to hand. However, there are some simple methods for forecasting the weather:

PINE CONES

These make a great weather forecasting tool as they will close up to protect their seeds in damp, humid weather ahead of rain and open back up when weather is fine. Try this yourself by hanging up a pine cone outside, near a window.

'RAINBOW IN THE MORNING GIVES YOU FAIR WARNING'

This lovely little saying is pretty accurate, as the weather usually moves from west to east. The Sun rises in the east so when rainbows appear opposite the Sun, this is usually a sign that rain is in the west and on its way.

'IF SWALLOWS FLY HIGH, THE WEATHER WILL BE DRY'

There is truth in this saying, too, as in good weather, the warmer air rises and insects are swept up higher into the sky, which means that insect-eating birds will fly much higher to feast on them.

ANIMALS AND BIRDS

Both are said to react negatively to poor weather. For instance, if a cockerel is restless and crows at night, rain is said to be on its way. We have a large cockerel at home called Rupert, who has been crowing at night recently; funnily enough, we have had so much rain that there has been some localised flooding. Next time I hear Rupert during the night I will wear wellies to work.

CREATE YOUR OWN WEATHER TREE

A weather tree is a beautiful way to record the climate.
The idea was developed by American writer Nora Waln in
the 1920s.[36] During her stay with a Chinese family, Nora was
invited to work on a painting of a plum tree whose branches
acted as an annual meteorological record. This painting was
called 'Chart of the Lessening of the Cold'. Today, you can buy
weather tree templates online, or make your own. To do so:

1. Take a large sheet of paper (e.g. A3), a marker pen and a
   selection of coloured pens, pencils or crayons.

2. Using the marker pen and paper, draw the bold outline of a
   tree with twelve branches – one branch for each month of the
   year and big enough to hold twenty-eight to thirty-one leaves
   (depending on the number of days in the month).

3. Choose a coloured pen or pencil to match a particular type of
   weather. For example, thunder could be purple, snow and ice
   could be silver while sunshine could be yellow.

4. Depending on the type of weather that day, select the
   corresponding pen or pencil and draw the outline of a leaf on
   the branch for that month.

5. If there's room, write the maximum and minimum temperatures
   in the leaf outline. If there's not, write these down next to it.

6. In this way, a weather tree not only monitors the changing
   weather but creates a colourful piece of art. I've made my own in
   the past, and they become wonderful keepsakes.

HOW DOES THE WEATHER AFFECT US?

Studies have shown that our behaviour actually changes with the weather. It's been found that warm temperatures and torrential rain increase aggression and irritability, and that violent crime is more likely to take place when temperatures soar. We are more likely to feel road rage when it's hot and also more likely to retaliate to another person's actions.

So, what about a dull day? How does this make us feel? In general, although our mood lowers with a dull day, it's actually easier to think clearly on these days. On a cloudy day we have increased concentration and focus, but the lack of sunlight lowers our serotonin levels, which lowers our mood. When this happens we can crave carbohydrates, but consuming these can make us lethargic – which means the concentration benefits brought about by a grey day are then lost.

Sunny weather has also been found to boost our creativity and make us more open to new ideas. The number of hours of sunshine we receive has an impact on our optimism and it seems we are generally nicer people in nice weather: we are more likely to tip for service, and feel romantic. A study in France found that hitchhikers were more likely to be picked up on a sunny day than on a dull day.

So it seems that, in some instances, warmer weather literally makes us warmer as individuals. One interesting experiment asked people details about themselves while holding a cup of liquid, and it was found that those holding the warm cup were much friendlier than those holding a cold cup. In fact, holding a cold cup of liquid was found to actually make people feel lonely.

Cold temperature affects our muscles so carrying out physical tasks becomes more difficult. I know that if I come into the office after I've got cold outside, I can barely move my fingers to type, they are so stiff and slow. Some days when I'm outside in the winter, the wind is so sharp, it physically hurts: the increase in atmospheric pressure moves bodily fluids from our blood vessels to tissues, which causes pressure on our joints and nerves that can lead to pain and stiffness.

Visitor numbers often fall at the arboretum on a rainy day, as many people simply don't want to get wet. However, I often work with groups in the rain; in fact, as long as you have the right clothes on, there is nothing more soothing than listening to the sound of rain or watching it fall. I love the sound of driving rain on windows, the pitter-patter on the car or on our tent as we camp. Listening to the sound of rain can lead to a state of calm, helping us to relax and sleep better. Many people liken it to white noise, as it allows us to fixate on purely the thought of that sound and everything else seems to melt away. It's incredibly mindful. Some think it relaxes us as it reminds us of being in the womb, soothed and safe.

'Let the rain kiss you. Let the rain beat upon your head with silver liquid drops. Let the rain sing you a lullaby.'

LANGSTON HUGHES, POET

THE SMELL OF RAIN

Humans are programmed to find the smell of rain attractive, as our earliest ancestors would have relied upon their ability to smell it in order to survive. We would have instinctively needed to look for fresh water to drink.

The earthy scent that rain gives off is called petrichor and is caused by multiple chemical reactions: when the rain hits the dry ground, bacteria reacts and gives off a pleasing scent. Plants also produce oils when they are dry and when rain falls, the smell of these oils is released into the air.

Thunderstorms can be frightening, but they can also have a relaxing effect on us too once they pass over. I always know when a storm is on its way because I get a thunderstorm headache caused by the sudden change in pressure created by the temperature changes in the atmosphere. Once we have the storm the air seems clearer and fresher – and my headache is gone and I feel good. The aftermath of a lively storm is not just a clear head but a huge release of those beneficial negative ions in the air we breathe, balancing our body, purifying our blood and boosting our immune systems.

'Some people feel the rain, others just get wet.'

BOB MARLEY

A RAINY DAY PICK-ME-UP

A rainy day reminds us that we are alive, so next time it rains
pop on your wellies and go for a walk, find some gratitude
and appreciation for the rain and what it actually gives to us.

Feel the rain upon your skin, you're alive.

Find the fun and splash through some puddles.

Listen to the rain falling perhaps on the pavement, your hood
or umbrella, or on the leaves in the trees.

Notice the drops of rain that gather on plants and leaves –
what shape are they? How do they form, change and move?

Breathe in the scent that rain gives off and smile.

SNOW DAYS

Most rain actually starts its journey to Earth as snow. High up in the clouds, snow occurs when there's moisture in the air and temperatures are low enough for tiny ice crystals to form, which then stick together in hexagonal snowflakes. Each snowflake has a unique pattern, nature's geometry being simple yet spectacular. These snowflakes melt into raindrops as they fall through warmer air in the atmosphere. However, when they are heavy enough and the temperature is cooler, they fall to the ground as snow.

There are few things better than opening your curtains on a winter morning and seeing crisp, freshly fallen snow. Being the first to step foot in the vast white space where no one has gone before you brings about a mindfulness all of its own. Snow in the arboretum turns the place into a magical winter wonderland, a Narnia where it feels anything can happen.

Snow has a calmness and peacefulness about it; everything seems so still and quiet when snow is falling and lies fresh on the ground. It inspires our sense of wonder, our imagination and makes everything look different. There's something very tranquil about a snow scene, the gentle fluttering of the flakes, the dullness in the air as the sky seems so still, thick and full.

Yet there can also be a childlike wonder, as schools close, roads grind to a halt and snow days are forced upon us. Where we live, people come together whenever it snows – neighbours clear each other's drives and families play together, building snowmen and dragging their pink-cheeked children around in sledges, spending quality time outside and making memories together.

Snow has a powerful fierceness about it too: it can stop us in our tracks, or cut us off completely. If you've ever experienced a blizzard, you'll know how it can make you feel lost and confused, when everything looks the same and it's a complete whiteout. In Russia, during late winter, the authorities spend every day recovering the bodies of the homeless from the streets when the snow starts to thaw. Chillingly, they call these dead 'snowdrops', after the first flowers to emerge after the snow in the spring.

A DEADLY BEAUTY

Avalanches are deadly layers of snow that move downhill at terrifyingly fast rates – speeds of 80 mph can be reached in five seconds. They can wipe out entire settlements and cause huge devastation.

Natural triggers include heavy snowfall falling in layers on steep slopes and a raising of temperatures that causes the surface snow to melt. Wind is also a major factor as it can cause drift snow and unstable top layers of snow.[37]

Humans can also trigger avalanches through mechanical movement or vibrations, winter sporting activities and deforestation. However, trees can provide a natural brake, slowing the flow of snow, and, when planted above settlements, can actually save lives.

WINDY WEATHER

Wind not only has an impact on snow, it has a major impact on our lives too. The strongest winds ever recorded in the UK have been on mountain tops in the Cairngorms with winds reaching speeds of 173 mph, while the windiest area of the UK is the Shetlands. Winter is the windiest time of year in the UK, when the jet stream tracks further south which allows more storms from the Atlantic to affect us.

The wind's speed, direction and gusts can be measured using an anemometer, of which there are many different types – from a basic homemade one using cups, right through to sonic types used by meteorologists. These plot a wind speed measurement on the Beaufort Scale, devised in 1805 by Sir Francis Beaufort, a Royal Navy officer. The scale was created for naval officers who made regular weather observations which were often quite subjective: one man's 'gentle gusts' could be another man's 'stiff breeze'. The original scale went from zero to twelve and wasn't a measurement of wind speed as such but of wind conditions and the effect of these on boats' sails. It wasn't until 1916 and the start of steam travel that anemometers came into use. The scale was extended up to seventeen in 1946 for tropical cyclones that affected Taiwan and China. Today we tend to measure the wind in either kilometres per hour or miles per hour, although gales are still often described as Beaufort Scale 8 or 9.

In the arboretum, the forecast of strong winds makes everyone nervous, as we have to close to visitors for safety reasons. I've had many sleepless nights pondering what awaits us after gale-force winds during the night, wondering which trees may have succumbed and fallen, and what damage awaits from broken branches smashing to the ground. But it's not all negative; the wind also excites me, it's a great movement of energy and blows away the cobwebs.

Not much research has been done into how wind affects us, but school teachers will tell you that children have an increased amount of energy when it is windy: they bounce on their chairs and become more fidgety in the classroom. Some schools allow for more outside playtime on windy days so that the pupils can release some of their pent-up energy. But it's not just people that are affected by the wind; animals can be too. My animals always act giddy in the wind; the dogs get zoomies and race around and the cats puff up like balls and run sideways everywhere with their backs arched. The chickens aren't as impressed as pecking is a little harder than usual in the wind when you're made of feathers.

LISTEN TO THE WIND

The sound the wind makes through the trees and leaves is called psithurism and has a hugely calming effect on our minds. Listening to the wind and watching the movement it creates can therefore be a very mindful activity. I often sit and close my eyes and just simply listen to the wind while I'm in the woods: it's an incredibly powerful form of meditation because as you are 'actively listening', it's quite easy to not get attached to passing thoughts.

When I watch the wind moving in the trees, it's almost like it's dancing with them – from the gentle swaying of the evergreens to the fluttering of each individual leaf on a branch. My daughter Lilith and I like to blow dandelion clocks into the wind and watch how far they sail, the wind being vital for some plants' seed dispersal. The wind has a mysteriousness about it: it's invisible, yet we can see its effect; we know it's there as we can feel it, yet we can't actually see it.

It's set to become windier in countries like the UK – again, that's down to climate change. As the temperatures increase Atlantic storms will be pushed towards our country, causing more stormy weather systems, which will no doubt have an effect on our seasons as we know them.

CELEBRATE THE WIND

**Take a few moments on a windy day to connect mindfully
with the currents of air that move across our planet:**

LISTENING TO THE WIND

Find a quiet place to sit or stand on a breezy day, then close your
eyes and take a few deep, slow breaths to centre yourself and relax.
Simply listen.
Notice how the wind moves and changes.
Is it close by or is it far away?
Notice the sound it makes as it moves
through the branches of the trees.

WATCHING THE WIND

Find a place to sit or stand on a breezy day, and
notice how the wind creates movement.
Let your gaze follow the sway of trees or the fluttering of leaves.
Notice the gentle movement it creates, the flow.

WALKING ON THE WIND

On a breezy day go, for a walk.
Have an intention to allow the wind to blow the cobwebs away.
Open up your senses and breathe.
Enjoy the freshness and invigoration the wind gives.

WHAT IS YOUR FAVOURITE SEASON AND WHY?

· ·

· ·

HOW CAN YOU USE SEASONS AS INSPIRATION?

· ·

· ·

HOW DOES DIFFERENT WEATHER AFFECT YOU?

· ·

· ·

· ·

· ·

· ·

WHAT ARE YOUR REACTIONS TO THE EXERCISES IN THIS CHAPTER?

· ·

· ·

· ·

· ·

· ·

Plants

4

As you have probably guessed, plants have always played a large part in my life. As a little girl, I remember the first house I lived in that had its own lawn, and how I would spend time with my grandfather, watching him prune his roses and grow vegetables — his tomatoes and cucumbers were legendary. While I later studied horticulture, and now work at the arboretum, my passion for all things green goes even deeper than that. My garden has always been my sanctuary. I love growing herbs and seeking out interesting plants and flowers for their scents, colours and textures. It has never mattered to me how small the space is, I've always managed to fill my garden with plants that excite me.

Plants feature in all our lives more than we may realise, and although our relationship with them has evolved over time, it is vital to our existence. They appeared on the planet long before humans. The earliest plants ever to exist were thought to be a type of green algae that formed in the ocean about one billion years ago. It wasn't until around 700 million years ago, when the Earth was predominantly rock, that the first plants appeared on land. Mostly mosses and types of algae, these early plants were non-vascular (without vessels to carry food or water), and didn't have deep root structures. Some scientists blame them for the formation of the Ice Age: in that period, Earth's temperature would have been around 120°C, owing to the amount of carbon monoxide in the atmosphere, and plants cooled the environment by releasing oxygen into the atmosphere. However, this in turn provided a pathway for other lifeforms to exist on Earth.

The first vascular plants appeared 400 million years ago, while the first recognisable soils appeared 350 million years ago, paving the way for the plants we see today. Given that humans didn't appear until a mere five to seven million years ago, the Earth really does belong to the plants – not us.[38]

Humans and plants share similarities in our DNA, research having found that we share around 1 per cent of our human genome with them. It's thought that genetic material from plants passed through our ancestral DNA via bacteria.[39] We really are part of nature.

Plants remain key to our wellbeing and our survival; we depend on them and we interact with them every single day directly and indirectly, be it through respiration, culture, clothing, medicine or food. Some 20,000 years ago, we used our hunter-gatherer skills to find the food we needed to eat, and it's now thought that the majority of our Stone Age diet would have been plant-based. Our digestive system resembles that of an ape, in particular that of the chimpanzee and orangutan, both of which enjoy diets rich in plants.

A WORLD OF PLANTS

I often wonder what the world would be like if plants reclaimed the planet. Ross Island is an abandoned British settlement in the remote Andaman archipelago, where plants have indeed taken back the land. Many of the island's landmark buildings and structures are covered in the roots of the Ficus tree: churches and buildings of what was once a colonial penal outpost are covered in twisted, knarred roots.

More recently, the Chernobyl nuclear disaster in 1986 turned a once bustling land into a 1,000 square-mile exclusion zone. Unlike humans, plants have learnt to adapt to the nuclear catastrophe, and within three years of the reactor meltdown they were recovering and re-growing over the land. Animals are back living in the area, and although their life spans are shorter than they might be elsewhere, the area is more abundant in plant life and wildlife than ever before. Wolves, wild boar and elk roam the streets, wandering past abandoned buildings thriving with plant life.

It seems to me that the only thing that stops plants in their tracks is us — and it is clear that we have a relationship with plants that goes even deeper than perhaps we realise. We need plants, but do they really need us?

ANCIENT WONDERS

Let's begin by looking at some ancient yet beautiful organisms that are easy to find and whose apparent simplicity belies how useful and fascinating they are: moss, lichen and fungus. In fact, two of these – lichen and fungus – are not, strictly speaking, plants at all.

MARVELLOUS MOSS

As we have seen, moss is one of the oldest plant forms. Lush and green, the very texture of moss invites you to touch it. Mosses can be found globally, except in saltwater environments, and as they always grow in clean atmospheres their absence is a good indication of pollution. They produce spores instead of seeds and don't flower.

This wonderful little plant has probably been used by humans since we first evolved. Sphagnum moss is particularly useful to humans, as it absorbs water from the atmosphere as well as the soil, and is capable of holding up to twenty-six times its own weight in water.[40] In extreme survival situations, the water in it can be wrung out and drunk, and as moss is acidic, this tends to be free from harmful bacteria. This wonderful moss is also a key component in fighting climate change: with its ability to store more carbon than any other plant, we could make a great change to our world if we allowed it to grow freely. Water moss, or *Fontinalis antipyretica*, was similarly used for its water-retaining properties by rural communities to transport water and extinguish fires; the Latin name when translated means 'against fire'. Moss can also be used to filter water, and indeed some green spas and swimming pools use the filtration qualities of moss to cut down on the uses of chemicals in their water, which results in cleaner air, purer water and fewer cases of irritated skin.[41] As well as holding water, moss makes a great dense insulating material for a shelter roof, retaining heat when it's cold and keeping the interior cool when it's warm.

Sphagnum moss is also naturally antiseptic and antibiotic, and wounded deer have been known to drag themselves over beds of sphagnum to aid their recovery. Reindeer eat a diet rich in moss as the chemicals within the plants help keep their bodies warm, whereas at the other extreme (in terms of habitat), sloths move so slowly that moss actually grows on their bodies, adding to their camouflage. They also feed it to their young, which they carry around with them – a bit like having a constant picnic.

When used dry, sphagnum can absorb fluid faster than any cotton wool and has been used throughout history by different cultures as a soothing wound dressing. In the two World Wars, moss was sometimes used in hospitals to treat injured soldiers, soaking up bodily fluids faster than any other type of dressing and, when soaked in pressed garlic juice, having life-saving antiseptic properties.[42] In Lapland, infants' cradles were traditionally lined with moss, creating a warm, clean, and dry environment for babies. This versatile plant has been used by many different cultures, including Native Americans, Europeans and Eskimos, to make nappy linings, as its absorbency prevents and heals nappy rash.[43]

GROW YOUR OWN MOSS

I once decided I'd like to have a few more stones in my garden that were covered in moss, so I decided to grow my own. In fact, growing moss is a very simple process and it's great if you want to 'age' a garden ornament or a stone wall.

First, find some starter moss. Take a look around your garden or when you are out and about: you will be surprised where moss grows once you start noticing it. Carefully remove a clump (with the landowner's permission if necessary). Alternatively, you can buy many varieties of fresh moss online or in specialist garden centres.

Place the moss in a bowl or blender and add buttermilk or natural yogurt. Mash up or blend the mixture until it starts to look like mud.

Use an old paintbrush to spread the mixture where you would like moss to grow.

In a few weeks you will have glorious moss growing where you didn't before.

MAKE YOUR OWN MOSS BATHMAT

My dream is to create a garden one day with a perfect moss path, where the moss is so thick it comes away in large clumps and the ground bounces beneath each footstep you take.

Why not have a go at bringing beautiful moss flooring into your own home by creating a living moss bathmat? To grow your own, you will need:

Large piece of card to create a bathmat template

Marker pen and scissors

2 large pieces of thick, dark-coloured, high-density foam

Enough pieces of moss to cover the mat (sourced locally or bought)

Sharp knife

Silicone sealant

Water spray

1. On the card, draw a template for the bathmat in the size and shape that you would like your mat to be. Cut out the template out and draw round it on both pieces of foam, then cut around the markings. Both pieces should be an identical size when you lay one on top of the other.

2. Remove the top layer of foam and arrange your pieces of moss in small sections on it. Then draw round them. Remove the moss, and carefully cut out the drawn shapes with the knife. (You can place each piece of moss back on the matching cut-out piece of foam, so that it's easier to work out what goes where when you are ready to construct the mat.)

3. Apply silicone sealant to the top cut-out layer and then press this layer onto the bottom layer of the mat, making sure each section and the edge of the mat are properly sealed, while wiping away any excess sealant.

4. Weigh down the mat using a heavy book or other item until the silicone sealant has dried (being careful not to stick the weight to the mat).

5. Prep the mat by misting the surface with the water spray. (You can also use commercially available moss adhesives.) Plant the moss by inserting each piece into the matching cut-out shape in the top layer.

6. Mist the mat while the moss is getting established. The moss may thrive on the run-off from your bath or shower water, but depending on the variety, you may need to water it occasionally to keep it happy. And finally, you're able to stand on it and use it.

LUMINOUS LICHENS

Many will know lichen as those colourful patches that appear on trees, rocks and stone walls. However, these bright smudges can also grow on soil, manmade materials and even on animals. Lichen will grow on pretty much any surface where it has access to light and moisture. That said, the saying that 'if lichen is growing, it means clean air' is absolutely true. Like moss, a lack of lichen is a reliable indicator of poor air quality, as its lack of roots and leaves mean lichen relies on the air to absorb the nutrients it needs to survive, and poor air quality means a lack in nutrients.

Curiously, lichen is not a single organism but a joining of fungus and cyanobacteria in a symbiotic relationship. Some lichen is edible, some can be used to make dye and a lot of different types have various medicinal uses and have been used to treat conditions ranging from arthritis and alopecia to leprosy and infections.[44]

When fungus is in season, I can often be seen foraging for mushrooms or, as some fungi are very poisonous, simply admiring their colours and variety – from the large saucer-shaped caps that sit in the parklands and huge brackets of fungus bursting high up on the stem of a tree, right down to small scarlet elf cups and the tiny, perfectly formed mushrooms that seem to trickle down bark.

The fungus kingdom is a whole world of living organisms in its own right, with over 100,000 different types. Fungus can live anywhere: in the air, in soil, on plants, in water, on animals and even on the human body; think of athlete's foot! Some fungus is edible and medicinal; Ötzi the Iceman, the wonderfully preserved mummy of a man who died over 5,000 years ago, was found to have a birch fungus in his possession, which would have been used for its antibiotic properties. However, other types of fungus can be deadly, such as the aptly named death cap and destroying angel. There are fungi that can be devastating in the form of crop destruction, while others can be life-saving in the production of antibiotics. Whatever their relationship to us, fungi are vital to the ecosystem, playing a key role in the breakdown of organic matter and formation of soil structures, nutrient cycling and exchange.

The toadstool or the mushroom is the fruit of a fungus and produces its spores. The mycelium, or the bootlace-like map that generally is hidden underground, is where the magic happens. This is the vegetative part of the fungus, the part that spreads and absorbs water and nutrients; this is also the part that in some types of fungus sends nutrients and messages to other plants in a symbiosis which we still know relatively little about (see Trees, page 73).

PLANTS AS FOOD

Regardless of what kind of diet you enjoy, plants very likely make up a significant part of it, offering a vast range of nutrients in the form of vitamins, minerals and phytochemicals. The recommended quantity of plants that you should consume in your diet to keep you fit and healthy varies depending on your age and fitness, but it falls in the region of five servings a day. Interestingly, research has discovered that people whose diets include seven or more servings of fruit and veg a day tend to be happier and enjoy better mental health.[45]

Plants are grown commercially all over the world for food; however, of the 20,000 edible plant species available, we only use about 150 of these, of which about twelve constitute three-quarters of the world's food. These include mega-crops such as sugar cane, rice, corn and wheat. Grains are particularly heavily produced, as they feed livestock as well as humans; however, it takes between 3 and 9kg of corn to produce 450g of beef through feeding the animal that it comes from.

Plant domestication has evolved over millennia. Very early farmers sowed seed from wild plants close to their homes and then collected the seed from the tastier or more prolific plants to sow the next year; and so the cycle continued. Over the generations, some species of plants have become genetically altered, changing into the crops with which we are familiar. For example, *Oryza rufipogon* is now considered to be a noxious weed in the States, but is the ancestor of *Oryza sativa*, or rice as a know it today. The ancient ancestor sheds most of its seeds before harvest and has large anthers for cross-pollination, whereas most modern rice species have fertilised seeds before their flowers even open. The changes in some plants' genetics following domestication means that many of our modern plants would be unable to compete in the wild and have become as dependent on us as we are on them.

With a growing world population, there is more need than ever for plants to feed us, and with the environmental challenges we are facing, plant conservation needs to be dealt with on a global scale to ensure that everyone has access to nutritious food.

FIVE FABULOUS VEGETABLES

When trying to ensure my family gets their five a day and the best nutrition they can from what I feed them, I try to mix it up as much as possible to please everyone's tastes. Here are some of our tried-and-tested favourites:

Spinach: the cartoon character Popeye's favourite has to be one of the healthiest leafy vegetables on Earth: spinach can provide over 50 per cent of your recommended daily allowance (RDA) of vitamin A and your entire RDA of vitamin K in one cupful. This amazing green leaf also has powerful antioxidants which help keep disease at bay, is great for keeping our hearts healthy and has been said to be full of anti-cancer benefits. Antioxidants reduce the number of free of radicals (the unstable atoms in the body that play a part in disease and aging), thereby reducing inflammation and protecting our cells from damage. I buy frozen spinach and throw it into whatever I'm cooking to add that extra healthy bang to our meals. It's also a great way of hiding the presence of veg from those with little tricky taste buds.

Kale: not only will a cup of kale provide you with your entire RDA of vitamins A, C and K, it also provides essential B vitamins, potassium, calcium and copper. Like spinach, it's packed with antioxidants, making it a disease fighter and great for healthy circulation. I have a habit of putting kale in everything and it's also my tortoise's favourite food – it's good to know that me and my tort share a healthy habit.

Carrot: whether eaten cooked or raw, the humble carrot always goes down a treat in our house. This easy-to-grow veg is packed with vitamins C and K. The popular saying that carrots can make you see in the dark contains an element of truth, as these veg contain high amounts of vitamin A, an essential vitamin which helps produce the pigment in our eyes that allows us to see in low light. If you had a vitamin A deficiency, you could develop night blindness which could be corrected by eating carrots.

Kohlrabi: this weird and wonderful vegetable is also known as the turnip cabbage. It is a relation of wild cabbage that looks a little like a tight ball of cabbage with unruly shoots of hair, and can be eaten cooked or raw. When eaten raw, this wonderful veg is packed with fibre and is full of vitamin C. Studies have found that it also has properties that reduce inflammation and lower blood sugar.

Beetroot: the leafy parts of this versatile vegetable are great in salads and packed with calcium and magnesium, while the deep-red spherical roots are high in fibre, vitamins B and C, and are a great source of potassium and iron for heart, muscle and bone health. Beetroot juice is a fantastic exercise enhancer as it's loaded with oxygen-improving nitrates which, when drunk, have been found to enhance sporting performance – much better for us than drinking chemical-laden, sugar-filled so-called 'energy' drinks.

Finding a good balance between your fruit and vegetable intake is important as fruit is just as high in all the good stuff. In fact, it can sometimes be easier to get fruit into our diets as they make great snacks and are more pleasing to those with a sweet tooth. I add fruit to my breakfast every morning in the form of berries, along with nuts and seeds, to give me that all-round nutrient hit. Fruits grow on many plants and bear the plant's seeds, which are often edible for humans and animals. Symbiotically, they not only provide food and nutrition for animals but they also use them as a way of seed dispersal. Here are a few of my favourites:

Oranges: these golden orbs are one of the most nutritious fruits you can find. Packed with minerals, they are high in vitamin C and citric acid, which help us to absorb iron.

Blueberries: this tasty form of superfood is easy to add to breakfasts or smoothies, or to enjoy as a snack. Loaded with vitamins and minerals, blueberries are especially high in antioxidants. These amazing little berries have the power to ward off chronic disease and boost our immune systems, and they have been found to be beneficial for our brains too.

Avocado: botanically speaking, the avocado is a berry with a single large seed. It's full of fibre, potassium and magnesium. Rich in healthy fats, this teardrop-shaped fruit has great benefits for our heart and blood.

Olives: technically a fruit, olives are a great source of vitamin E and are full of minerals such as iron, copper and calcium. They're also great for our heart health.

Tomatoes: not to be confused with a vegetable, this fruit contains seeds and is produced from a flower. Tomatoes are packed with fibre and vitamins, are full of powerful antioxidants, are great for keeping our hearts healthy and good for our skin too.

A TASTE FOR TEA

Besides being cooked in meals, plants make delicious healthy drinks and smoothies – and teas. My eldest daughter Freya and I often meet for green tea dates, when we catch up and put the world to rights over a pot of the good stuff. While the leaves for green tea are picked from the same plant – *Camellia sinensis* – as those used to make black tea (which we call 'builder's tea' in our family), they haven't undergone the same withering process. Black tea is oxidised while green tea is not.

Considered by many to be the healthiest beverage on the planet, green tea is brimming with nutrients and antioxidants, making it a great detoxing drink. It is also good for brain function, as while it contains caffeine, there is less than in coffee so your brain can reap the benefits without the jittery feeling. Studies have found that the effect on our brains of green tea can help lower the risk of Parkinson's and Alzheimer's later on in life.[46]

One of the earliest records of tea drinking dates to the third century CE in a Chinese medical text. The Japanese tea ceremony – known as the Way of Tea – originated in China, and was first practised in Japan by Zen monks, who drank tea to keep themselves awake during long periods of meditation. The practice gradually spread to daily use and the Japanese tea ceremony was developed to greet and honour guests and friends. The Wabi-cha style of tea ceremony takes place in a dedicated tea house, a small structure made from rustic materials with a low door. There is sometimes a fire pit for heating the tea kettle, a scroll on the wall, flowers for decoration and an array of rustic tea utensils.

The ceremony has strict qualities:

HARMONY, both between the attending guests and between the utensils used;

RESPECT, between the guests but also for the utensils and the ceremony itself;

CLEANLINESS, in that the tea house must be thoroughly swept and cleaned before the ceremony and the guests must wash their hands and rinse their mouths before entering;

TRANQUILLITY, which is shown through the caring use of each part of the ceremony.

I suppose the British national love of tea is another type of ceremony; when we invite people into our homes, the first thing we usually do is to offer them a warming, welcoming drink.

MAKE YOUR OWN HERBAL TEA

Tea can be made from a variety of widely available herbs, such as mint, basil and chamomile. You can even use cleavers or goose grass, those sticky stems that straggle over hedgerows, traditionally used by herbalists for tackling water weight gain. Simply pick your own, shake out any insects, wash and steep the leaves or flower heads for a few minutes in hot water, strain and then serve. Add a teaspoon of runny honey for extra sweetness.

Herbal teas don't just taste great, but they can have health benefits, too. Herbs have been used in teas for thousands of years by cultures all over the world for their medicinal and healing purposes. Mint, for example, has been used traditionally to aid digestion and soothe cold symptoms.

PLANTS AS MEDICINE

Plants have been used as medicine since prehistoric times, and about 40 per cent of our medicine today comes from the plant world.[47] I often think about those first, early people who discovered the uses, benefits and cures offered by plants: the trials and tribulations of finding which ones were beneficial may have been eventful – or was it instinct perhaps? Did we just know? Maybe our sense of smell told us which were good for us in an age when we were more in touch with ourselves. I'm fascinated by the health benefits of plants, which are so often overlooked. Of these, herbs offer some of the simplest and most readily available home cures.

HEALING HERBS

Herbs have fuelled my own love of plants; I suppose it comes down to my nursing background and my interest in plants as medicine. In Britain during the Middle Ages, monks cultivated great physic or herb gardens. Part of their daily routine included working in these gardens, where they grew plants for food, medicinal and spiritual use. The crops were used to benefit their local communities as well as themselves.

Growing your own herb garden is simple and enjoyable to do. Many herbs will grow easily from seeds, which can be bought from most good garden centres. If you don't have much space in your garden, try growing your herbs in flowerpots or indoors on the windowsill instead. Be aware of the climate you live in, as some herbs won't thrive in the cold.

Here are a few handy
suggestions to get
you started:

Lavender: this purple-flowered beauty makes a great addition to any herb garden, attracting butterflies and bees. It is easy to grow in a border as a low hedge or in a pot, and can be used medicinally, cosmetically, as flavouring in foods and as a tea. It is anti-inflammatory and antiseptic, as well as anti-fungal and anti-viral. It's also great for boosting the immune system and the scent is calming and good for promoting sleep (see Aromatherapy, page 214).

Mint: this old favourite is very easy to grow but can become an invasive pest if not kept in check. Why not grow some in a pot close to the kitchen, where it is accessible and can be kept under control? Mint can be used medicinally, in foods and as a tea.

Chamomile: this cheerful little plant is easy to grow in a pot, as a border or even as a lawn or seat. Walking upon or sitting on chamomile will release a wondrous scent that soothes and calms the mind. This herb can be used medicinally, cosmetically and as a relaxing tea.

Rosemary: this shrubby evergreen does better in a border as it can grow quite large, but it can be grown in a pot. It is used medicinally, cosmetically, in food and as a tea.

Lemon verbena: this attractively scented woody plant isn't suited to a frosty area, so here in North Yorkshire we grow ours in a pot and bring it indoors to overwinter. (I can't stop myself having a squidge of the leaves whenever I come across this plant, as the smell is irresistibly tangy.) It can be used medicinally, in food and as a tea.

DANDELION DELIGHT

You may be surprised by the plants that can be used as herbs; it's not always the beautiful and most fragrant and can include some contenders that could be considered weeds. Most people in the UK will be familiar with the humble dandelion as a lawn pest, but this little yellow wonder is one of the most important early flowering plants to grow in this country, providing pollinating insects such as bees as well as beetles and hoverflies with vital resources in the spring when emerging from hibernation. It's also eaten by some types of caterpillar.

If you really don't want dandelions in your own garden, I would at least urge you to wait until just before the flowers go to seed before you remove the blooms, so those little bugs stand a chance. That said, the seeds of a dandelion are an important early food source for some small birds, such as sparrows and finches. And it can also be food for us: every part of the plant is edible.

The uncooked leaves are packed with vitamins A and C, calcium, magnesium and iron, and, like spinach and kale, are loaded with antioxidants. Bitter in taste, they are great in salads, although some people may find them more palatable if picked before the plant flowers. While bitter-tasting leaves are part of a plant's natural defence against being eaten, we can benefit from this: bitter foods stimulate the liver to produce bile, which emulsifies fats and makes nutrients such as vitamins A, D, E and K more available. In this way, the taste can also calm hunger.

The leaves can also be eaten as a vegetable and some cultures boil them and use them in soups. They contain a powerful diuretic, treating urinary disorders and fluid retention without dehydrating the body; hence the old wives' tale that you would wet the bed if you picked a dandelion (reflected in the French word for them, *le pissenlit*). They are also a great blood cleaner and detoxifier, and can be used to boost iron levels for those suffering from anaemia.

The flowers can also be eaten and make a bright, healthy addition to a salad. They can be baked into cakes and made into wine, while dandelion flower buds can be pickled or added to omelettes and flowers. Even the pollen can be used to sprinkle on food for decoration. The white sap that oozes from the stem if snapped can be used to treat corns, warts and verrucas. The long tuberous tap roots, while notorious for being difficult to remove, deserve to be thought about in a different light. Full of nutritional minerals, they can be eaten, pickled and even roasted to create a substitute for coffee. They contain a magenta dye that can be used for wool and their medicinal properties range from treating anything from a headache to heartburn, reducing inflammation, right through to acne. All this from the little yellow bloom that grows in our gardens, which may not be such a pest after all.

WILD AT HEART

Whatever the size of your garden, if you are wildlife lover consider re-wilding a little area of it. Let the weeds grow and encourage a variety of plant life. Scatter wildflower seed and perhaps leave small areas of lawn to grow long: don't be afraid to let the grass go to seed.

As well as enjoying wildness in my own garden, we have a large area of wildflowers and long grass at the arboretum. Each year, its rewards are slightly different: it may be the appearance of a different wildflower that has decided to make the meadow its home or it may be the sighting of an insect not previously seen in the area. Whatever it is, it is always the most beautiful of surprises.

THE KITCHEN MEDICINE CABINET

The use of herbs, spices and plants as medicine can be traced back to ancient Egypt, where their use was documented in the ancient Ebers Papyrus.[48] With over a hundred pages, this scroll dates back to *c*.1550 BCE, and is thought to be copied from an even earlier document. The manuscript lists in detail hundreds of remedies and formulas, including a large number of plant-based remedies. Some of the ingredients will be familiar today, including mint, poppy, basil (for its benefits to heart health) and garlic.

GARLIC

Closely related to the onion, the garlic bulb is used by many in cookery for its strong flavour. However, you should consider including these amazing cloves in your diet for their health benefits as well. Known for its immune system-boosting properties and blood-cleansing abilities, garlic is mildly antibiotic and great for treating the common cold: studies found that people who took garlic supplements during a cold or flu had reduced symptoms and recovered more quickly than those not taking garlic.[49] Garlic lowers blood pressure and cholesterol and reduces clotting. It also contains antioxidants.

TURMERIC

The root of this aromatic plant can be ground into a vibrantly coloured spice and used in curry dishes, and it has amazing health benefits too. In Chinese medicine, turmeric is used to stimulate the circulation, treat bruising and aid blood clotting. In Thailand, it is used as an anti-venom because of these same properties. Turmeric helps to clean the liver, while curcumin, a substance in the spice, some say has been found to kill cancer cells and prevent new ones growing. While more research is needed into this root, it is advised that turmeric be taken alongside other cancer treatments.[50]

ARNICA

This plant grows in Northern America, Europe and Asia in mountainous habitats. While the plant itself is toxic, medicines made from it have homeopathic benefits and it's a household favourite of ours: arnica cream can be applied to skin to treat bruises, sprains, swellings and muscular pains, while arnica tablets relieve muscle pain. Arnica was once prescribed (alongside other treatments) by a vet for our dog Bibi, to help ease the inflammation and aid healing after she got bitten by an adder.[51]

CABBAGE

When I breastfed my children, I suffered from mastitis on a number of occasions and while I took antibiotics, I also used Savoy cabbage. A midwife friend advised me to pop a leaf into my bra on the affected side to ease the discomfort, which I did – and it worked! Cabbage contains certain compounds that are anti-inflammatory. So simple and such an effective remedy.

POT MARIGOLD (CALENDULA)

This orange bedding plant brightens up the summer garden and can be grown between vegetables to ward away pests. The leaves and flowers of the common pot marigold or *Calendula officinalis* can also be used in salads or as a garnish. The plant is antiseptic and antifungal and contains vitamin A. When taken internally, it helps cleanse the liver, lower fevers and reduce inflammation. It can also be used as a skin treatment to reduce pain and swelling, and can be applied to nappy rash, to chapped lips or as an anti-fungal cream. It has been found to help promote new tissue growth and is also thought to reduce Sun damage and the appearance of scars. It even makes a good insect repellent.

CALENDULA CREAM

I love making this cream, and sometimes like to add a handful of dried lavender flowers to the infused oil for their healing and soothing properties, or, if I'm making a beauty balm, rose petals for their toning and hydrating qualities. To make a simple calendula cream of your own, you will need:

50g dried calendula flowers (bought ready dried or, if you grow your own, picked early in the morning and allowed to dry)

100ml high-quality carrier oil, e.g. almond, coconut or olive oil

Approx. 600ml hot water

15g beeswax

10-20 drops of essential oils of your choice, e.g. soothing lavender

Clean jars

1. First, add the dried flowers (and any other flowers if using) to the carrier oil. Either leave the mixture to infuse for several weeks or, for quicker results, heat on low in a slow cooker for 12 hours before allowing to cool overnight. Strain the flowers from the oil once cooled. The mixture should be a rich yellow colour.

2. Pour the hot water into a blender and set to one side. This is to prevent the mixture from sticking to the sides of the blender when you come to use it.

3. Create a double boiler by placing a heatproof bowl inside a saucepan of water (making sure the water does not rise over the rim of the bowl). Place the beeswax and infused oil inside the bowl and gently heat, stirring as the beeswax melts. Once the beeswax has melted, remove from the heat and add your essential oils.

4. Empty the water from the blender into a jug and add the oil and wax mixture to the blender. Put the lid on the blender but leave the filler cap off. Blend on a slow speed and gently pour in the warm water. You may need to pause and scrape down the sides of the blender to make sure all of the water is absorbed.

5. When the mixture has emulsified, pour it into the clean jars and allow to set. The calendula cream can be kept for up to a month in the fridge.

ECHINACEA

This beautiful perennial belongs to the daisy family and is easy to grow, with stunning pinkish-purple cone-shaped flowers that attract butterflies, bees and dragonflies. It is high in antioxidants and believed to have incredible immune-system-boosting properties: if taken in a tincture, some argue it can halve the chances of catching a dreaded cold or flu virus and speed up your recovery if you do fall ill. It can also help to lower blood sugar, reduce inflammation and anxiety.[52] It is great to use during winter months when croup, coughs, colds and bronchiolitis strike. I buy it in a simple tincture form and add the drops to water. I also like to drink echinacea tea.

ROSE

Rose hips are high in vitamin C and are a powerful antioxidant, and the tea tastes nice too – I drink a cup myself every day and grow wild shrub roses in my garden, *Rosa rugosa*. They create a great natural barrier, have beautiful scented blooms and then display their huge scarlet hips after they've finished flowering. It's been found that smelling roses lowers blood pressure and cortisol levels, reducing stress. The scent can also relieve depression, anxiety and help you get a better night's sleep. To make a simple cleanser, mix powdered rose petals with some water and honey to make a paste and apply this directly to the skin for a great uplifting cleanse – or why not make your own rose water?

ROSE WATER

Rose water has a variety of uses and is one of my favourite things to make. It is known for its hydrating properties and is a great toner, good for relieving puffy eyes. You can also add a cup of it to your bath water for a calming, soothing soak, or use it to flavour food or drinks for that floral hint. It can even be used as an effective yet gentle mouthwash, and as a hair rinse for added shine. To make your own, you will need:

1 cup of fresh rose petals or
½ cup of dried petals

5 cups of filtered water

1. Add the petals and water to a pan and bring to the boil before turning down the heat.

2. Simmer for 10 minutes, until the petals' colour fades.

3. Allow the mixture to cool completely before passing it through a fine sieve.

4. Decant into clean jars and store in the fridge for two weeks, sealed, and use for cosmetic or culinary purposes.

There is another way of making rose water for cosmetic (but not culinary) purposes which gives longer-lasting results. You will need:

12 drops of high-quality
rose essential oil

1 teaspoon vodka

1 cup of distilled water

Mix the essential oil and the vodka together. Add to a clean jar with the water. Store in the fridge, sealed, shaking before each use.

AROMATHERAPY

Aromatherapy uses aromatic plant extracts to benefit health and wellbeing, but while it has been used by our ancestors for centuries in various guises, it wasn't formally recognised as a therapy until relatively recently. During the First World War, French perfumier René-Maurice Gattefossé was working in his lab when he burned his hand. He plunged it into a large jar of lavender oil and was astounded by how quickly it healed afterwards, thereby discovering the healing properties of the plant. He went on to experiment with their healing benefits and to treat injured soldiers using essential oils, which is when the term 'aromatherapy' was first used.

I diffuse essential oils at home and, besides calming lavender (see page 203), I have a couple of old favourites, which I use in different combinations, depending on my mood or situation:

FRANKINCENSE
This magical resin comes from the sap of a tree that grows in Africa and Arabia, and has air-purifying properties. It can be used to enhance moods, relieve stress, and improve memory and concentration. It's also great for relieving congestion and eases breathing. I love its earthy, woody smell.

SWEET ORANGE OIL
This uplifting oil would give an energising boost to anyone's day.

PEPPERMINT OIL
A refreshing scent that is great for getting rid of a headache in minutes and soothing nausea when diffused into the air.

'How could such sweet and wholesome hours
be reckon'd, but in herbs and flow'rs?'

'THE GARDEN',
ANDREW MARVELL

PLANTS IN THE HOME

How do we feel when someone gives us flowers or a plant? A living gift has the ability to heal a wound, brighten a space or send a message. My son, Elliot, once gave some Calendula plants to a great friend of mine, who planted them in her garden. These bright flowers are the gift that keeps on giving, setting seed each year. Every time I visit when they are in bloom, I am reminded of our friendship, its deep meaning and the impact my friend has made not only on me but on my children.

I love displaying fresh bunches of flowers in my house, which I pick from my garden and the surrounding woodland, including what some would call weeds poking out from the mix of flowers and foliage. Flowers not only brighten the house but lift the day.

Plants have been making their way into our households for almost as long as humans have had homes; between 400 and 500 BCE Egyptians, Romans and Greeks were all documented as growing indoor plants, which symbolised wealth and were often used to decorate palaces and temples. In the Far East, the Japanese and Chinese developed the art of bonsai, bringing miniature trees inside. In eighteenth-century Britain, glasshouses were the privilege of wealthy households, in which they showcased tropical plants.[53] In modern times, most people have some kind of pot plant growing either in their homes or at their place of work. Plants and flowers make us feel good, change the feel of our living space and brighten up dark corners. They bring life and energy into quieter rooms, and peace and stillness into hectic work spaces. Best of all, they are good for us.

House plants help improve the air quality, and with most modern buildings having heating and air conditioning, it's nice to know we can enjoy an element of freshness even when indoors. Certain plants such as spider plants, mother-in-law's tongue and chrysanthemum are particularly known for their air-purifying properties. House plants can also help raise humidity levels, fight dust and protect us from respiratory issues, sore throats and dry coughs. Plants placed in the bedroom have been found to help us to sleep better: a pot of lavender can soothe even the busiest of minds when night time comes.

Feel-good factors are huge with house plants; they have been found to reduce our blood pressure and lower heart rates, and to reduce stress and anxiety. When placed in school environments, they can aid concentration levels and attention spans, while studies have found that plants placed in hospitals help recovery and reduce pain.[54] Research repeatedly comes back to plants being good for us in all manner of situations; their therapeutic benefits are quite simply amazing.

'If we could see the miracle
of a single flower clearly,
our whole life would change.'

BUDDHA

THE LANGUAGE OF FLOWERS

Given their many benefits, it's perhaps not surprising that plants and flowers have been used as important symbols by different cultures for thousands of years; the Bible, the ancient Greeks, Egyptians and Chinese all refer to flowers in their stories and legends.

While gifts of flowers took off in Britain during the Victorian era, the English adopted an entire language of flowers from Turkey in the 1700s, and this, along with a growing interest in botany, sparked a floral revolution. Floriography, or the language of flowers, fast became a craze, with nearly every flower being assigned a meaning or multiple meanings taken from the respective plant's characteristics and behaviours:

CALENDULA OR POT MARIGOLDS

According to the Language of Flowers, these have a message of cruelty – although I am pretty sure this was the last thing on my son's mind when he gave some to my friend! I will perhaps think twice now about which flowers I give as gifts.

MOCK ORANGE FLOWERS

A bouquet of mock orange denotes a message of deceit.

MOSS

It's nice to know that if I were to hand over a gift of moss, I would be sending a message of love and charity – I think from now on everyone will be receiving mossy stones from me!

ROSES

The red rose has long been a symbol of love. According to the language of flowers, a closed rosebud symbolises new love and to give one red rose symbolises love at first sight. However, a gift of a rose can also symbolise that the receiver is still the giver's one true love. To give six red roses is said to mean infatuation, to give fifteen symbolises an apology, whereas a gift of a hundred red roses suggests a devotion unlike any other. A white rose signifies innocence, purity and perhaps secrecy; a yellow rose symbolises joy and friendship, a dark pink rose is a thank you and deep crimson is given when in mourning.

In the language of flowers, to give a bouquet of sweet peas is to say goodbye.

LEGENDS OF THE ROSE

The rose is a timeless flower that features in many myths and legends around the world. It was probably first cultivated in ancient China and then grown widely in the Middle East during the Roman period. In ancient Greece, Aphrodite, the goddess of love, was said to have created the red rose, which sprang from the ground where her tears and drops of her lover Adonis's blood fell. In Hindu legend, Lakshmi, the goddess of prosperity and good fortune, was created from 1,008 small red rose petals and 108 large red rose petals. In Arabic myth, it is said a nightingale fell in love with a white rose and pressed itself up against the flower, where a thorn pierced its heart and the bird's blood turned the white rose red.

THE COMMUNITY OF PLANTS

The difference a horticultural environment can make to a person is immensely rewarding. The confidences built and friendships made over plants can be incredible, and the calming atmosphere that plants create really is nature's balm. Using horticulture as therapy is an age-old tradition although perhaps few of us realise it; most people will say they feel uplifted or perhaps de-stressed and relaxed after having a good old potter in the garden.

Using plants as therapy is also a subject very close to my heart, as on leaving nursing I went to work initially for Horticap, a wonderful charity that provides a working environment for students with learning and other disabilities.[55] It's a safe setting where people can thrive. I was employed as a horticultural instructor and my job was to support the students in the daily running of the nurseries.

REMEDY

GROW YOUR OWN GREEN FINGERS

There are many organisations such as Horticap and open gardens which need volunteers – and getting involved can be a great way to get your own nature fix.[56]

Why not look in your local area and volunteer in a garden to lend a much-needed hand and get a dose of natural goodness?

In more recent years, I have enjoyed working regularly with groups, introducing them to the healing world of plants. Every time I do a community project or a show garden and people are brought together, I see the wonders that evolve: the freedom, the friendships and the achievement are addictive.

I recall a particular group that I worked with in the arboretum from our local Help for Heroes recovery centre, Phoenix House, in Catterick. The guys and girls undertook to build a small educational garden at the arboretum and it was amazing to watch their confidence grow as their ideas were brought to life, and see the calm that had come over the group by the end of a day.

Another year, I joined a group of veterans from Phoenix House in building a garden at the RHS Chelsea Flower Show. This was a completely different ball game: the busy, pressured world of show gardens perhaps wasn't very calming but it was inspiring; we had fun, we worked hard and we stood back to look at the finished garden with pride, knowing that we had all done our bit. Our garden went on to win a silver medal and the People's Choice award. Even better, one of the veterans in the group has since completed his horticulture certificate and is now working in a large garden and enjoying his new career.

I completed another military-related project, which saw a large memorial garden being built for my local flower show, the North of England Horticultural Society's Harrogate Flower Show, which went on to win gold and Best in Show – a huge achievement for the group who helped build it. Afterwards, the garden was relocated to a military base as part of a large project, designed to create a tranquil space for soldiers and their families to enjoy. Like most military camps, this base was functional and a bit soulless, so the garden made for a simple yet very effective way to lift spirits and boost health. After all, a military camp isn't just a place of work for serving soldiers, it's a way of life for whole families and greening these areas no doubt boosts the quality of that life for these exceptional people.

Gardening and plants bring people together. I volunteer as a judge for Yorkshire in Bloom, whose winning entrants go on into the Britain in RHS Bloom competition.[57] You'd be forgiven for thinking it's all about the floral display, but it's so much more than that. As judges, we look not only at the horticultural practices, the environment and the educational value, but also the community engagement. I love visiting villages and towns, and seeing community projects of all shapes and sizes come to life as people pull together, taking pride in their local natural environment and securing its future for generations to come. The smallest project can enter and be recognised in this sort of competition – which I believe should be encouraged, as these kinds of projects can help open people's eyes and reconnect them with nature.

'A garden is a grand teacher.
It teaches patience and careful watchfulness;
it teaches industry and thrift;
above all it teaches entire trust.'

**GERTRUDE JEKYLL,
HORTICULTURIST AND GARDEN DESIGNER**

OPENING OUR EYES TO PLANTS

A few years ago, I attended a lecture on a phenomenon called plant blindness; this is when people are simply not aware of the plants around them.[58] Studies have shown that most city dwellers cannot name more than a couple of wildflowers, and that the problem starts with children in education. Lessons on botanical subjects are few and far between, which leads to generations of children who have little knowledge of the world in which they live; a disconnect then forms and these children grow up with little care and respect for the very world that supports them. With little importance being put on plant science, education and careers, the knock-on effect is a lack of experts who can in turn become world leaders in researching food shortages, medicine, plant pests and diseases, climate change and global warming. In higher education, the decline in courses run worldwide is alarming and you can no longer enrol in a botany degree in the UK.[59]

We need to make plants important again: we owe it to the future of not just the planet but of the human race, too, to do so, because if we don't, it's not just the natural world that will suffer – we will as well. So why not begin now, by starting a project, building a community – and bringing people together for the future of our world and the wonderful plants we share it with?

WHAT DO PLANTS MEAN TO YOU?

. . . .

. . . .

. . . .

WHAT WAS THE LAST PLANT YOU REALLY NOTICED?
WHAT DID IT LOOK LIKE? CAN YOU NAME IT?

. . . .

. . . .

. . . .

TAKE A LONG LOOK AT THE PLANTS THAT FEATURE IN
YOUR EVERYDAY LIFE. WHAT DO YOU NOTICE?

. . . .

. . . .

HOW MUCH OF YOUR DIET IS PLANT-BASED?

. . . .

EXAMINE A PLANT IN DETAIL – IT COULD BE A PLANT IN YOUR
HOUSE OR YOUR GARDEN OR ONE THAT YOU PASS EVERY
DAY ON YOUR WAY TO WORK – WHAT DO YOU SEE?

. . . .

. . . .

Birds, Animals & Insects

5

If somebody were to ask us to think of an animal, most of us would probably think first of familiar creatures such as dogs and cats, cows and pigs, or perhaps something exotic like a gorilla or a whale. However, while we're sitting there, busily listing all the animals we can imagine, it might not occur to us to look in the mirror.

As we go about our daily lives, it can be all too easy to forget that humans are animals too and part of the wider animal kingdom in all its incredible diversity: from humble sponges on the seabed, insects clinging to the underside of leaves, to our fellow primates, and the birds soaring in the skies. I often like to remind people that we are already a part of nature; we just need to rediscover our connection with it. And where better than by exploring the world of animals?

THE CRADLE OF LIFE

I have heard and read so many different theories about how humans evolved, from the sacred to the secular. The scientific evidence suggests that animals first appeared on Earth about 800 million years ago in our oceans in the form of sponges and jelly-fish-type creatures.[60] Oxygen was still at relatively low levels on the planet, including in the oceans, and creatures like these need very little oxygen to survive. Scientists have struggled to determine from which of these two life forms animals first evolved, and while it was originally thought to be the jellyfish creatures, it's now thought more likely that humans evolved from sponges.

THE MIGHTY SEA SPONGE

Sponges are plant-like animals. They are made up of cells, fibres and water that surround skeletal parts, but they don't have a brain, heart, nerves, muscles or a mouth. They come in all shapes, sizes, textures and colours, and they don't move. Their bodies are full of tiny pores through which they pump water, filtering food particles. These seemingly simple creatures have an amazing ability to regenerate themselves and, impressively, can recreate a whole adult from just a tiny fragment – even a single cell.

There are around 5,000 to 10,000 different types of sponge, the majority of which live in salt water and cover our ocean floors. Sponges are valuable members of the ecosystem and are vital components of the great ocean reefs. Alongside corals and other marine life, they play an important role in nutrient cycling and oxygenating our beautiful oceans.[61]

Humans have been harvesting sponges for thousands of years; the ancient Greeks used sea sponges for domestic cleaning and cosmetic use, while Greek athletes used sponges to apply olive oil to their bodies before competing. Ancient Egyptians also held the humble sponge in high esteem and used it during the embalming process, when the sponge would be soaked in perfumes and oils, and used to clean the body of the deceased.

Some cultures still rely heavily on harvesting sponges; in fact, this form of aquaculture has been conducted on a commercial scale globally for many years. Today, sponge farming is a major business in Florida, where there are now laws in place to secure its future. Divers used to collect the sponges using a hook method, where the sponge was hooked and ripped free. However, this method was found to damage a sponge's chances of regrowth, whereas a cutting method greatly improved the sponge's chances of re-growing. The law states that sponges must be harvested using only the cutting method and some areas are protected from sponge harvesting entirely.

Perhaps not surprisingly, overharvesting remains a cause for concern. Many other animals rely on sponges to survive: they create habitats for a number of fishes, crabs, worms and other marine life; they provide food too and are the primary source of nutrition for the beautiful and critically endangered hawksbill sea turtles that are found in tropical reefs.

JELLYFISH – THE OCEAN'S COLOURFUL DRIFTERS

Whether watching them in the wild or an aquarium, there are few things more hypnotic than the dance-like movements of a jellyfish as it drifts through the water. The colours, translucency, patterns and shapes are mesmerising.

Jellyfish aren't fish but are in fact relatives of corals and anemones. Like sponges, they don't possess a brain, heart or bones and consist mainly of water. Around 2,000 different types of jellyfish have been identified, although marine biologists believe there may well be hundreds of different types out there with which we aren't yet acquainted.

Around seventy of the known species can be harmful to humans. Most jellyfish have stinging tentacles to capture prey and defend themselves. When food or a threat presents itself, the jellyfish triggers an action that forces the sting to release a venom that paralyses its prey or causes pain to a threat.

It is therefore one thing to spend time peacefully watching jellyfish, but quite another to swim with them. While on holiday in Tenerife, my daughter Freya was suddenly surrounded by a bloom of jellyfish in the sea: hundreds of hand-sized pink jellyfish with tentacles as long as her forearm gathered around her. She was stung by what felt like tiny spikes on the tentacles and likened the pain to being similar to a nettle sting but much, much worse. She had a nasty rash for a few days but the pain subsided quite quickly after she left the water. The sea was rapidly evacuated by officials but the jellyfish then found themselves washed up on to the shoreline. There was then a mass effort by everyone on the beach to get them back in the water before they died, and the animals were carefully returned to the ocean where they belonged.

Although species such as the box jellyfish and the Irukandji jellyfish are notorious for the strength of their venom, not all cultures fear jellyfish. The animal is seen as a delicacy in many Asian countries, while dried jellyfish can be used as an organic fertiliser.

Jellyfish numbers are on the increase, which some believe is caused by climate change and overfishing, fish being the jellyfish's natural predator. The increase of jellyfish blooms is a sure sign of the deterioration of our marine ecosystem. In addition, the growing numbers of wind farms and gas and oil platforms have created the ideal habitat for jellyfish, as the young ones like to attach to downward-facing solid surfaces, which are harder to come by in the natural world.[62] A great number of blooms have been detected in the Adriatic Sea, which is also where the number of sea platforms has increased from a handful in the 1970s to over 150 in the present day.

Now that jellyfish have officially been labelled a 'nuisance species', it is perhaps no wonder that people are researching uses for this over-population. Besides acting as food, it is thought this ancient underwater angel could hold some of the answers to our energy and plastic problems in the future. A compound called green florescent protein (GFP) which occurs naturally in jellyfish can be used as a marker in cell and gene biology, and is also being researched as a possible future energy source by scientists in Sweden.

Science is also looking to jellyfish to solve the plastic problem in the oceans. Used in products ranging from cosmetics to cleaning products, microbeads are tiny balls of plastic that don't degrade or dissolve, resulting in a mass plastic crisis in our waterways world-wide, killing marine animals and causing damage to the ecosystem and environment. Many countries have now banned the use of these devastating beads, but they are still present in our seas. Encouragingly, studies have shown that jellyfish mucus binds to microplastic, so in the future jellyfish-like filters could be used.[63]

The lifespan of a jellyfish can vary from a few hours to, well, forever. There is one jellyfish that doesn't die: the immortal jellyfish. Once these jellyfish reproduce, instead of dying they return to the juvenile phase; their bodies shrink, their tentacles retract and they sink back down to the ocean floor, where they start their interesting life cycle all over again and again, over and over. The only known way by which this determined creature can die is by way of disease or being eaten.

Another sea creature with tentacles that I am particularly fond of is the octopus, and after listening to an interview with naturalist Sy Montgomery, author of *The Soul of an Octopus*, I think I may love them more than ever. I have only ever seen these fascinating creatures in aquariums, but when you look at an octopus it's like they are really looking back at you and figuring you out. They seem to have distinct personalities: some look cheeky, some look bold and others quite shy. They can glide as gracefully as jellyfish but with an added spark of speed if needed and a ripple to their moves.

Like squid, the invertebrate octopus is a cephalopod, from the Greek for 'head, foot'; given that they appear to consist of a head and limbs, this nomenclature really does make sense. Octopuses are highly intelligent animals. Their ability to escape through tiny spaces, to open jars, untie knots and release ink when in trouble are among their most well-known tricks; but they can also use tools, play with toys and display emotions. They can change colour to camouflage themselves, inspiring naval scientists to study the way they seemingly disappear into their surroundings.[64]

Like sponges, they can regrow lost limbs; however, even their limbs have brains of their own, of sorts: while their main brain sits inside their heads, many of their neurons are in their eight limbs, meaning that they effectively have nine brains. It has been found that each limb has a personality of its own, with some arms coming across as brave and some as quite shy.

There are over 300 different types of octopus and they are usually quite solitary creatures, living alone in dens; but while we may think they are unfeeling animals, it seems that perhaps they do feel in ways similar to us. Octopuses change colour when angry, excited, scared or relaxed; they also have a version of oxytocin – known as the 'cuddle' hormone – in their systems, which may suggest that they are more social than we realise.

FROM LIVE-GIVING SPONGE
TO THE MIGHTY WHALE

The earliest fish appeared 530 million years ago, while the first animal with a backbone was a strange eel-like fish similar to the modern lamprey. Fossil evidence suggests that 500 million years ago, animals began to explore the land; these were most likely amphibious creatures that lived primarily in water but came on land to avoid predators, or to mate.

Around 480 million years ago, insects evolved at the same time as terrestrial plants began to appear. Early reptiles started to appear some 300 million years ago, and then came the major splits in evolution: mammals start to appear and reptiles started to evolve into dinosaurs and then birds. Two hundred million years ago, the reptiles were the dominant animals on land and in the sea and air. Mass extinction over sixty million years ago wiped out most of the large reptiles, paving the way for mammals.

Mammal evolution then splits, as some developed on land while others went on to develop back in the water; the earliest confirmed primate fossil dates back to around sixty million years ago while the ancestors of whales started to appear fifty million years ago.[65]

The earliest whales lived in the oceans but returned to the land to give birth to their young, and it took another ten million years for them to return entirely to the ocean.

Today, blue whales are the Earth's biggest mammal, growing up to 30 metres in length. If you think that the average human is 1.7 metres tall, you'd have to get seventeen of us to stand on top of each other to get to the same length. Blue whales can weigh a whopping 180 tonnes; again, with an average human weight of 70 kilograms, 2,667 people would be needed just to balance those massive scales. That's pretty impressive.

Throughout the ages, whales have featured in myth and legend, with many civilisations fearing this aquatic giant. In ancient China, it was believed that a great whale-like creature with human hands and feet ruled the oceans. In Hawaii, whales are seen as sacred, and beaches where whales are washed up are regarded as sacred ground.

Yet since ancient times, humans have exploited whales for their meat, oil and bones. The whaling industry flourished between the sixteenth and nineteenth centuries, when the human 'need' for the oil produced from the animal was at a high: whale oil was used for fuel, for making textiles, for soaps and for lubrication. During the World Wars, whale oil was used in the production of explosives and later, during the 1960s, it was seen as a viable source of vitamin D.

It wasn't long before sport and entertainment became a factor, too, with the first killer whale or orca being caught and displayed in 1961, only to die approximately forty-two hours after her capture. Commercial demand increased for whales in captivity when it was found that these intelligent animals could be 'trained' to perform tricks. A catastrophe occurred in 1970, involving the cover-up of a mass capture and the deaths of orca, which thankfully led to the Marine Mammal Protection Act being passed in 1972.

Whales are intelligent, social animals that deserve the utmost respect.[66] They live in family groups known as pods and travel together, migrate together, play, learn and communicate together. Scientists have found that, like the octopus, they are conscious beings with large brains.[67] We should be learning from them, not making them our playthings.

LISTEN TO THE SONG OF THE OCEAN

Whale song has mystified humans since the 1960s and 70s, when biologist Roger Payne and his wife, Katy, first began to record the calls of a male humpback whale. It's now known that different whales sing different songs, with individual pods developing their own songs and learning tunes from each other.

Whale music has perhaps unfairly gained a reputation as a bit of a New Age cliché, but anecdotal evidence suggests that it is very soothing, and can help calm women during childbirth, soothe crying babies, aid meditation and promote deep sleep.

To experience it yourself:

Download or purchase a recording of whale music – there are lots of recordings available online.

Make sure that you won't be disturbed.

Switch on the recording.

Lower the lights or close your eyes.

Lie or sit in a relaxed position, allowing the sounds to flood your body and the tension to drift away.

Make yourself aware of your surroundings, surface to consciousness – or allow yourself to drift off to sleep.

OTHER WATERY WORLDS

If you don't have the opportunity to explore the heart of the ocean, there are plenty of different creatures to be found living along our shorelines and in our waterways if you take the time to look.

Rock pooling has been a favourite pastime of mine since I was a little girl; there is little more mindful than carefully and quietly searching a pool for signs of life – the dart of a fish, the scuttle of a crab or the gentle sway of an anemone. My favourite creature to find was the hermit crab; if you found one and looked closely you would see its tiny claws blocking the mouth of its shell to protect itself. However, if you were patient enough they would pop out to take a look around. When I take my own children rock pooling, I try to teach them to be as quiet and calm as possible when searching; it's an activity that you can be quite absorbed in for hours.

I also used to spend hours as a child paddling in rivers and streams to see what I could find. It was always a treat to discover a minnow or a stickleback. Sticklebacks are little predators that feed on even smaller fish, tadpoles and other small animals; they are easily distinguishable by the spikes that grow on their backs. I was lucky if I could catch one in a jar to examine it more closely, as they darted about with such speed.

My brother and I would creep along a bank or wade very slowly, lifting the occasional stone to see what would dart from under it. We would often find leeches stuck to the upturned rocks. These segmented, worm-like creatures are hermaphrodites that live on a diet of blood which they 'leech' from their prey. But not all leeches are human bloodsuckers; in the UK, there are sixteen species of freshwater leech, which mostly feed on worms, molluscs and fish. Since ancient Egyptian times, leeches have been used in medicine, and leech therapy – or hirudotherapy as it is known – is still practised today. Leeches are well known for their abilities to help improve blood flow and circulation, and are used in plastic surgery and reconstructive surgery to help prevent blood clots and prevent tissues dying. No pain is felt by the patient as these clever little creatures administer a local anaesthetic at the same time.

KEYSTONE SPECIES

Time to take a large leap now from the humble leech to an animal that used to shape the course of waterways in Britain and Europe many centuries ago – the beaver. Although the beaver is native to Britain, it became extinct in the sixteenth century, when it was hunted for its fur, meat and scent glands, which were used in food and the production of medicine and perfume. However, in 2009, beavers were reintroduced in Scotland and they now have protected status. There are schemes to reintroduce them into England and Wales too.

The reintroduction of beavers in the UK is seen by many as being a positive move towards rewilding the country.[68] Beavers have a positive effect on the environment; they live in wetlands and coppice bank-growing trees and shrubs by gnawing at the stems. The resulting regrowth of these coppices provides habitats for insects and birds. Beavers are, in fact, a keystone species.

Keystone species are often dominant predators that are critical to the relationships within a particular ecosystem and which have a disproportionate effect on the other organisms within it. The removal of them can have a devastating effect on diversity and habitat, and in some cases whole ecosystems cease to exist. The reintroduction of keystone species to areas where they are now absent because of human actions is key to rewilding and aiding the environment.

WOLVES AND REWILDING

In 1990, Yellowstone National Park in America saw the reintroduction of the keystone species, the wolf – an animal that hadn't
been seen in the park for over seventy years.[69] Previously, the
federal government's predator control programme, designed to
manage so-called 'nuisance predators', had succeeded in wiping
out the grey wolf, which was already in decline when Yellowstone
was created in 1872.

In 1973, the Endangered Species Act was passed in the US, paving
the way for the reintroduction of the grey wolf, and thereby revers-
ing the impact that the loss of this top predator had had on the
whole ecosystem. Grey wolves hunt and feed on elk: with the wolves
removed, the elk had been free to dominate the landscape, grazing
on a diet of mostly aspen and willow. Beavers rely heavily on willow
as a food source during the winter, and with a lack of willows came
a lack of beavers. This in turn had a negative impact on the waterways, affecting the flow of rivers, the lives of the fish that swam in
them, bankside vegetation and songbirds and insects. The reintroduction of the grey wolf has seen a complete turnaround and is an
example of how and why we need to take care of all animal life on
the planet.

Wolves disappeared in England in medieval times due to hunting
and deforestation with a few remaining in Scotland until the late
1600s. It's believed that the reintroduction of wolves into Britain
could see a knock-on effect in which entire ecosystems are restored,
including those of healthy forests.[70] There appears to be little reason
why the wolf cannot live harmoniously alongside us, as populations
across the world suggest they pose little threat to humans.

A rewilding project taking place in an ancient woodland near
Bristol is giving researchers a chance to see just how reintroducing
keystone species may impact the environment. For the first time
in 1,000 years, the carefully curated Bear Wood project in South
Gloucestershire sees bears, lynx and wolverines living together in
their natural habitat.[71]

PRIMATES

Primates are another keystone species. These include lemurs, monkeys and apes and humans, who belong to the sub-group of primates known as the Great Apes, along with chimpanzees, gorillas and orangutans.[72] Besides having 98 per cent of the same DNA as our biological cousins, the Great Apes have a large and complex brain, molar teeth in the lower jaw, a shoulder structure that enables free movement of the arm, an appendix, a lack of tail and a ribcage that forms a shallow but wide chest.

Sadly, studies show human activities such as farming, the palm oil industry, logging, mining and deforestation are destroying the habitats of our primate relations. Over half of all primate species on the Earth are facing extinction, which will no doubt have a huge impact on ecosystems all over the planet.[73] If, for example, the gorillas disappear, so will the mountain forests in which they live, and if we consider the importance of trees in creating the conditions that allow life (see pages 73-119), we could perhaps be putting humans on that ever-growing list of endangered species through our own actions. We need animals just as much as we need trees and plants to survive.

THE END OF LIFE AS
WE KNOW IT?

Britain is home to over 70,000 different species, but sadly wildlife numbers have plummeted by around 60 per cent since 1970. With increases in aggressive agricultural practices, loss of habitat, pollution and climate change, these figures don't look like they will be reversed anytime soon. The wildlife loss in the UK mirrors what is happening elsewhere around the planet. Some experts believe this is the start of the sixth mass extinction on Earth – otherwise known as the Holocene extinction, which is believed to be primarily caused by human activity. A recent report by the National Biodiversity Network found that a quarter of the UK's mammals and nearly half of our birds are at serious risk of extinction; a heartbreaking situation.[74]

THE WILDLIFE ON YOUR DOORSTEP

Wherever you live, the chances are that you don't have to travel far to see some amazing wildlife. In fact, there is beauty of some sort to be found in every little beastie – from iridescent beetles living in the back of the coal shed to dust-bathing sparrows. Depending on what sort of native animal you wish to see, it's often just a case of patience and perseverance – and the occasional piece of luck. Even seemingly common creatures can turn out to be quite remarkable, such as one of my family's favourite birds: the humble pigeon.

PIGEON

Deemed a pest by many, this highly intelligent bird is really quite interesting once you get to know it. Pigeons can fly at speeds of up to 60 mph and they have incredible eyesight that allows them to see an object 26 miles away. They also have superb hearing and they are able to detect storms, earthquakes and volcanic eruptions. These social animals mate for life; when raising their young, both parents care for the squabs and are able to produce a milk -like substance with which they feed their young.

SQUIRRELS

Another animal often thought of as a pest (or the grey ones are at least), like pigeons, grey squirrels are one of the most visible forms of wildlife both in urban areas and in rural communities. They were introduced to the UK from North America in the 1870s as fashionable additions to large country estates. Little did people know that by introducing this innocent creature, they would threaten the native red squirrel.[75] The grey squirrel is a larger, more robust animal, which finds overwintering much easier than the more delicate red. They can also carry a virus called squirrel pox that is fatal to the reds; however the numbers of greys that carry this virus in the modern day are in decline.

When asked about 'problem grey squirrels' at a talk I was giving, my response was that they are now resident and naturalised. If we want to blame someone for their presence, it's not the fault of the squirrels themselves; they are just busily going about their daily lives. Curious and mischievous bundles of fun, they probably do a better job of planting trees than we do.

BADGERS

This stripy-faced nocturnal animal can often be glimpsed at dusk in woodlands and nature reserves. There is a badger sett (the den where they live) near my home and we often go out in the early evening in late summer to watch the family of badgers tumble and play with each other, groom and scrabble for food. If you discover a sett, you may be able to spot signs of their regular routes through the undergrowth nearby. It amazes me how close you can get to them without disturbing them. Their eyesight is quite poor but they have a keen sense of smell, so as long as you stay downwind of them, you should be able to watch them for a while before they set off on their nightly wanders.

HARE

These magical creatures feature a lot in folklore. Larger than rabbits, with long back legs and big ears, hares lollop around the countryside and are in fact the UK's fastest land mammal. The hare was first introduced into Britain by the Romans. Instead of living in warrens like rabbits, they live above ground and rest in shallow depressions in the earth known as 'forms'. They can often be seen boxing in spring, which occurs when a female fends off an overly persistent male; these furious displays have coined the term 'mad as a March hare'. Sadly, because of loss of habitat and human activities, these wonderful creatures are in decline, but they are protected by law and if you spot a hare you are encouraged to log your sighting with the Brown Hare Preservation trust.[76]

HEDGEHOGS

Sadly also in decline through loss of habit, these little prickly characters are most easily seen in the evening and are fascinating busybodies. They get their name from the fact that they like to live along hedgerows and grunt. I spent a number of years helping to rescue hedgehogs in Harrogate, and became fascinated by their unique personalities. Some were quite friendly, while others would hiss and headbutt you at any opportunity. If you would like to encourage hedgehogs into your own garden, you can leave suitable food and water out for them, create hedgehog highways between neighbouring gardens and even make a hedgehog house for them to live and breed in.[77]

BATS

The only mammals capable of true flight, and more agile than most birds, bats are fantastic creatures to watch when they emerge in the evening to hunt for insects. To encourage them into your garden, plant night-blooming flowers such as dahlia, French marigolds, and evening primrose, along with honeysuckle and thyme, to attract nocturnal insects, which, in turn, will bring the bats.

Evenings are generally a great time to spot wildlife; all kinds of creatures, such as foxes and owls, venture out at twilight in search of food.

WILDLIFE TRACKS

Why not take a crash course in wildlife tracking and learn the tracks that different types of animals make? Some animals can be quite hard to spot, so knowing how to read their tracks will help you to be more aware of their presence and on the alert to see them.[78]

The easiest place to spot tracks is in the mud or in snow. If you spot tracks, place a coin beside them as a form of measuring stick, then take a photo and look them up when you return home. Closer to home, put a tray of sand in your back garden to see what visitors you have overnight.

Always be respectful when spotting wildlife: keep your distance, stay quiet and calm and don't attempt to touch or disturb any animal or animal habitat.

AN EVOLVING RELATIONSHIP WITH ANIMALS

Humans have always had some form of relationship with animals; however, it has evolved over time. Finds have been made of spears used by early hunter-gatherers, while fossilised animal remains show telltale marks made by instruments that were used to remove meat from bone.[79] Prehistoric cave art found in France, Spain and other locations around the world depicts all kinds of different animals. While little is known of the meanings of these drawings, it's thought that early humans may have believed some animals were magical and that their art may have had spiritual significance. Ivory animal figurines have been unearthed that are believed to date back to the Ice Age; again, no one is sure why these figurines were carved – perhaps they were tokens of religious or magical belief, or perhaps our oldest ancestors just loved animal trinkets.[80]

THE DOMESTICATION OF ANIMALS

Between 2500 BCE and 13,000 BCE humans started to domesticate animals. Much like plant domestication, this would have happened over many generations, during which animals would have been bred for their desired qualities, whether for food or to aid hunting and pest control. It's thought that the first animal to be domesticated by humans was the dog from a wolf-like ancestor in around 10,000 BCE. The acceptance of dogs into human lives had a benefit for both humans and this canine, as the wolf-dog helped humans to hunt and they in turn rewarded it with a share of the food.

However, perhaps this early relationship with animals was about more than just convenience? A 14,000-year-old grave excavated by scientists was found to hold not only human remains but those of a twenty-eight-week-old puppy, which had died of disease. Not only have experts been able to tell what type of disease the puppy had, but that the dog was well cared for.[81] The fact that people cared for this puppy both while it was alive and on its death suggests an emotional relationship between humans and animals rather than only a working one.

'Dogs look up to us.
Cats look down on us.
Pigs treat us as equals.'

**SIR WINSTON CHURCHILL,
BRITISH PRIME MINSTER 1940–45; 1951–55**

HORSE SENSE
Wild horses were originally hunted for meat, milked and then domesticated around 6,000 years ago for agricultural purposes and for transportation. Taming these mighty beasts changed how humans travelled, farmed and communicated; after all, a message delivered by horseback arrived much quicker than a message delivered on foot.

In this way, they helped to bring communities together, but they were also used to pull them apart: horses were used in warfare by the cavalry and, as portrayed by author Michael Morpurgo in *War Horse*, for pulling heavy guns on the battlefield. Humans gradually started to view the horse as much more than just a beast of burden, and horsemanship became very much about a working relationship and emotional attachment with the animal. Today, the phrase 'horse sense' has become a synonym for common sense.

THE LOYAL DOG

Our relationship with dogs is a powerful one. Huge health benefits come from simply owning a pet: as well as the joy felt when greeted by someone who is always pleased to see us regardless, they encourage us to take exercise and people who have an illness or injury tend to recover quicker with a pet; as they tempt us to be playful and have fun, to be social. Playmates and protectors, they help us to unwind after a tough day.

While seen as unclean by some cultures, dogs and other canines have long been revered as sacred by others. The ancient Egyptians worshipped a deity called Anubis who had the body of a man but a dog-like head; he was the god of the dead and protected souls on their journey into the afterlife. In Native American cultures, Coyote is a canine trickster god who rules over the rain and is known for his funny, foolish and cunning behaviours.

Dogs continue to play significant roles in different cultures and religions. The Hindu festival of Tihar takes place over five days in November, during which time dogs, along with crows and cows, are worshipped and lavished with food, flowers and attention. It's believed that to care for or adopt a dog is a pathway to heaven.

Dogs have even been revered as saints. A thirteenth-century French legend describes how a knight went hunting one evening, leaving his baby son with his trusted dog, Guinefort. On his return, the knight found the nursery in chaos, the child missing and Guinefort with blood around his jaws. Believing his dog had harmed the child, he killed it, but then heard a child crying. When the knight looked under the upturned cot he found his son safe and unharmed, alongside the dead body of a viper. Realising that Guinefort had been protecting his child, the knight created a shrine for him. The local villagers started to visit the loyal hound's grave and to report miracles; Saint Guinefort became known as a protector of infants.

Over the centuries, dogs established themselves as vital members of the workforce in many professions and industries, from herding sheep to protecting our homes and saving lives, like the famous St Bernard, bred to rescue travellers lost in the snow-covered Alps. Today, dogs work in law enforcement alongside police officers, doing jobs that humans simply aren't capable of, such as sniffing out substances and finding missing people. They have also been used in warfare since ancient times, and are trained to serve in combat, and as scouts, trackers and sentries. They are still used in many different roles – from search and rescue to detecting land mines. Military working dogs are awarded one rank higher than that of their handler, as a traditional reminder that the handler should treat their animal with respect. To date, thirty-four dogs have received the **PDSA** Dickin Medal, the animal equivalent of the Victoria Cross, which is awarded to animals for outstanding work and bravery.

'For man, as for flower and beast and bird, the supreme triumph is to be most vividly, most perfectly alive.'

D. H. LAWRENCE, AUTHOR AND POET

Dogs also make fantastic assistance animals and are increasingly being used in therapeutic settings – from the famous guide dogs for the blind to helping people cope with all manner of disabilities, illnesses and conditions.

VOLUNTEER WITH ANIMALS

If you are an animal lover, but you don't have the space or time for a pet of your own, why not offer some help to one of the great animal charities that are out there?[82] Animal charities rely on donations and volunteers' time, and offer opportunities to work with a wide range of creatures – from working with or caring for dogs and cats, to equine-assisted therapy[83] – and even llama therapy![84]

Do a little research to find out which sort of voluntary work would suit you and is available in your area. With a little bit of commitment, you could soon start to welcome animals into your life in ways that will ultimately help them and others, as well as yourself. Studies have found that the benefits of having a pet range from increased exercise and opportunities to socialise, to decreased cholesterol and triglyceride levels.[85]

BIRDS

Few things can be as therapeutic as watching a sky full of birds or being in a woodland that is alive with birdsong. It's when I wander into the woods on my own that the wonder of birds is truly revealed to me; I slow down, I take my time, I listen and look. A feeling of calm comes over me and the longer I take to notice what is around me, the more is revealed.

I once stopped to listen to a woodpecker. It took time, patience and stillness, but I eventually spotted the red and black flashes high up in the canopy, where I found her. I watched her peck into the side of a tree trunk, looking for the grubs and insects. Then she flitted from tree to tree cautiously, observing every movement and sound. At last, she revealed her treasure: a nest hidden within a perfectly round hole not much bigger than the width of her body. Each time she approached it, I could hear the noises coming from her chicks. It was a precious moment that made me lose all sense of myself and my daily worries.

THE INSPIRATION OF BIRDS
Long celebrated and imitated by artists, writers and musicians, birds have also inspired developments in engineering, inventions and science. Take my woodpecker friend: this beautiful bird has the ability to peck twenty times per second and do this around 12,000 times a day – all without getting even a headache.

After suffering from concussion in a bike accident, designer Anirudha Surabhi looked to woodpeckers for inspiration when coming up with a new design for a helmet.[86] Using the unique structure of a woodpecker's skull as a starting point, he created a helmet that as a result is much lighter and safer than old models.

BIRDWATCHING BENEFITS

People became interested in birds in Britain during the Victorian era, a time of fascination in the natural world. Unfortunately, this fascination wasn't always beneficial to the birds themselves; they became a collector's dream, with many individuals acquiring large egg, feather and stuffed bird collections. It wasn't until the late nineteenth century that attitudes changed and birdwatching became a more popular form of appreciation, which remains so today.

A study carried out by experts in 2013 at the University of Exeter found that people living in areas with more trees and plants had lower levels of stress, anxiety and depression and felt much happier when they saw a bird.[87] It doesn't seem to matter what kind of bird is spotted or where it is, these feathered friends seem to have the ability to raise our spirits, making us feel happier and more connected to the world around us.

REMEDY

FEED THE BIRDS

I have bird feeders placed next to windows around our house. One feeding station is situated on the edge of the woods, which invites even the shyest of birds to come for some needed treats, which means we get to know all our feathered neighbours.

To bring birds into your own life, simply buy a couple of feeders and fill them with bird-friendly foods such as peanuts, black sunflower seeds and fat balls. (Avoid bread, which has no nutritional value for birds, and dry biscuits, which can cause them to choke.) Clean and replenish the feeders regularly.

Once you have started to encourage birds into your garden, you could take part in events such as the 'Big Bird Watching Event', or your local equivalent, and help monitor the population of wild birds in the country.[88]

BIRDSONG

Birdsong is often sung by male birds seeking to find a mate or defend territory – which doesn't seem particularly peaceful. However, it seems that listening to birdsong is nevertheless good for us: research has found that this sound has a positive effect on our brains.[89] As well as relaxing our bodies and reducing tiredness, these delicate notes stimulate our brains and make us more alert, more able to concentrate, and improve our ability to remember things. When Freya was in the middle of her exams, I advised her to study outside in the garden, and the cacophony of birdsong proved a great aid to her studies.

An experiment in a school in Liverpool found that when students were played a soundscape of birdsong and nature after lunch, they didn't suffer so much from that post-meal slump you get halfway through the day and were more alert and better able to focus on their studies. Alder Hey Children's Hospital in Liverpool has similarly adopted a nature remedy by playing birdsong in the hospital corridors to help calm and relax young patients. Amsterdam's Schiphol Airport likewise uses birdsong in their quiet lounge to help soothe anxious fliers.[90]

'I want to sing like the birds sing, not worrying about who hears or what they think.'

RUMI, SUFI POET

BIRDSONG RADIO

REMEDY

The next opportunity that you have, why not go outside and spend some time listening to birdsong? Notice the different songs and calls; close your eyes, find some peace and enjoy the music.

If you don't spend much time outside during the day, you can always download the RSPB Birdsong radio app (other apps are available) and take those beautiful sounds with you everywhere you go.

BIRDS AND THE ENVIRONMENT

Birds aren't just 'useful' to us in a therapeutic sense; birds, like the rest of nature, are vital for our very survival.[91] Seabirds, for instance, play important roles in maintaining the health of ocean reefs, by helping to fertilise these amazing ecosystems with their droppings.

Birds spread seeds as well, carrying them in their digestive systems. As they travel over seas and great land masses, they disperse the seeds of future plants in their droppings and potentially return plants that were once lost to their original ecosystems. Some 70 per cent of New Zealand's forests and plants have been seeded like this. In this way, birds have an ability to transform landscapes and by doing so keep ecosystems in check, thereby playing key roles in oxygen production on the planet. They also play a huge role in pollination, pollinating around 5 per cent of those plants that are used by humans for food and medicine.

Birds have another important part to play in our food: they consume between 400 and 500 million tonnes of insects each year that could otherwise be potentially devastating to our crops; they are a vital biological control. But that is not to say that we shouldn't give insects the respect that they are due: insects have been around in one form or another for the past 412 million years and are essential to the wellbeing of the planet.

SMALL BUT MIGHTY –
THE INSECT KINGDOM

There are over a million different species of insect on the planet. They are the most diverse group of animals and they make up about 80 per cent of the world's animal species, with more being discovered all the time. In the UK alone, there are around 24,000 different types.[92] They come in all shapes and sizes, with the smallest being the fairyfly at a teeny 0.1 millimetre, to the huge neo-tropical titan beetle at nearly 17 centimetres long.

Insects are essential pollinators, ensuring the fertilisation of flowers, which then results in the formation of seeds and fruit. Many different types of insect are pollinators, with bees being probably the most important as they pollinate a third of all the food we grow and 80 per cent of all flowering plants.

My youngest daughter Lilith and I love examining the bees in our garden as they go about their chores – from the fluffy bottom of the bumblebee to the smooth striped abdomen of the honeybee – while taking care not to disturb them, or get stung!

There are 20,000 different species of bee worldwide and 250 different types in the UK. By virtue of their role as pollinators, each type is tasked with sustaining life on Earth, yet these crucial flying insects are in rapid decline and a third of our bee population in this country is seriously affected.

The destruction of their habitats from urban development and aggressive agriculture, combined with the removal of woodlands and trees for those bees living in wooded areas and the indiscriminate use of pesticides, are all having an adverse effect on the bee population. Extreme weather caused by climate change is changing weather patterns and affecting our seasons, meaning flowering plants are having to adjust, which is also a cause for concern among our bee populations.[93]

Why not come together as a community and plant a bee corridor? I've seen this done in many villages and towns: it's a fantastic way for communities to come together to look after local wildlife. Very simply, everyone involved agrees to grow lavender in a pot or garden border, thereby creating a bee corridor. The lavender plants ensure that not only bees but all pollinators have a steady stream of food everywhere they travel through the community they share with you.

'If we die, we're taking you with us.'

THE BEES

CREATE A BEE-FRIENDLY GARDEN

It doesn't matter if you have a large garden or a windowsill,
everyone can do something to help the bees.
Like us, bees need the basics of food, water and shelter.
Plant flowering plants such as lavender to attract them.

Other good plant options include:

CROCUS

This flowering plant adds
an early splash of colour
in the garden, and can
be naturalised in lawns,
planted in the border
or grown in a pot. They
provide vital early food
for many insects, not just
bees. Although bees will
go to any coloured flower,
they prefer purple and
crocus come in a range of
fabulous purple shades.

BUDDLEIA

A firm favourite in many
a garden, this hardy
plant will grow in most
places, even the sides
of brick buildings and in
paving cracks. It produces
wonderful flowers in the
summer months and is a
hit with bees, butterflies
and hoverflies – all vital
pollinators. This plant can
grow large but is easily
pruned to keep it in check.

OXEYE DAISY

One of my favourites
and with a long flowering
period, this plant not only
looks great for much of
the year but also provides
food for insects for a
long time. This can be
grown in the borders and
looks lovely in a pot.

It's very simple to make a 'hotel' for bugs and bees. Simply fasten a small bundle of bamboo canes together and this will make as good a home as any if space is limited, or drill different sized holes into a log.

HAWTHORN

If you have room in your garden, this early flowering tree is a pollinator's favourite. It not only looks lovely but smells wonderful, too, and the berries in the autumn double up as food for the birds.

LIME

This is a tree, so it needs space, but it's a beautiful plant and a favourite with bees. We have a lime avenue in the arboretum; when the Sun is shining and the trees are in flower, the floral scent hangs in the air and the sound from the canopy is amazing – a loud hum of happy, busy bees.

BEAUTIFUL BUTTERFLIES

Most people love the sight of a butterfly fluttering past, as a reminder of sunshine and warmer weather. In the arboretum, we have a wildflower area that comes to life during the late summer months. The plants there attract pollinating insects, hundreds of different types of butterfly, bees, dragonflies and damselflies, helping to support their numbers.

Every five years or so, the Butterfly Conservation charity researches the numbers of the UK's butterflies. The report in 2015 concluded that not only are the UK's native winged beauties in decline, but numbers of migrating butterflies are down too.[94] Once again, the causes are thought to be habitat destruction, human behaviour and climate change.

Butterflies are easiest to spot around flowering plants. You can encourage them into your garden by planting butterfly-friendly plants such as red valerian, verbena and hebe, by creating habitats for them, or supporting the work of charities like Butterfly Conservation.[95]

THE IMPORTANCE OF CONNECTION

Our sense of connection to not only the bees but to all animal life is important, as we need to take their protection and preservation seriously or the outcome will be devastating for the planet. We can look to the natural world and the animals themselves to learn how a natural balance can benefit all.

Examples of animal symbiosis are everywhere when we know where to look, and they can take some surprising forms: different species of animals have been found to hunt together, such as the grey wolf and hyena, both benefiting from each other's skills.[96] Zebras enjoy the relationship they have with the birds that hitch a ride and eat the ticks on the zebra's skin, thereby feeding the birds and curing that irritating itch all at the same time; while crabs carry anemones around on their backs – the sea blobs hitch a ride while protecting the crab from predators.

Predators and prey can also coexist in surprisingly harmonious ways: tarantulas and frogs have been found to share a home in a mutualistic relationship. While the spider could easily kill and eat the frog, it doesn't: instead, the tarantula protects the frog from predators and offers it a food source from insects feeding on the remains of its prey; while the frog protects the spider's eggs from ants. It seems that during the 2020 bushfires in Australia, a wombat allowed other species of animals into its burrow to escape the blaze, offering them shelter and protection.

If we were to take a leaf out of nature's book and live in better harmony with other animals, that mutual support would no doubt filter through back to us. A shared love, care and respect for all living things that happen to co-exist on one planet.

MINIMISING OUR IMPACT

A report by the World Wildlife Fund for Nature carried out in 2018 describes how wildlife populations have declined by more than 50 per cent in the last fifty years.[97] It is clear that in the time that humans have been around on Earth, we have had more impact on the planet than any other species. The destruction of habitats, the presence of plastic in the oceans, the manmade noise all around us is having devastating consequences: birds are singing in the middle of the night because of false light, pollinators are avoiding areas because of human noise and sea creatures are dying because their stomachs are full of our waste products.[98]

However, we can all make a difference. If we take the time to notice the nature in our own lives, to connect with it and to do what we can to take care of it – for the wellbeing of ourselves and the future of this planet – these small steps will begin to take us a long way. From acting individually, we could even find that we are part of an incredible global collective, that we really are connected to this beautiful world around us.

HOW DO BIRDS, ANIMALS AND INSECTS IMPACT YOUR LIFE?

....

....

....

....

WHAT ARE YOUR THOUGHTS AFTER LISTENING TO BIRDSONG?

....

....

....

....

WHAT ARE YOUR THOUGHTS AFTER SPENDING SOME QUIET TIME JUST WATCHING THE LIFE HAPPEN AROUND YOU?

....

....

....

....

HOW CAN YOU MAKE A DIFFERENCE?

....

....

....

....

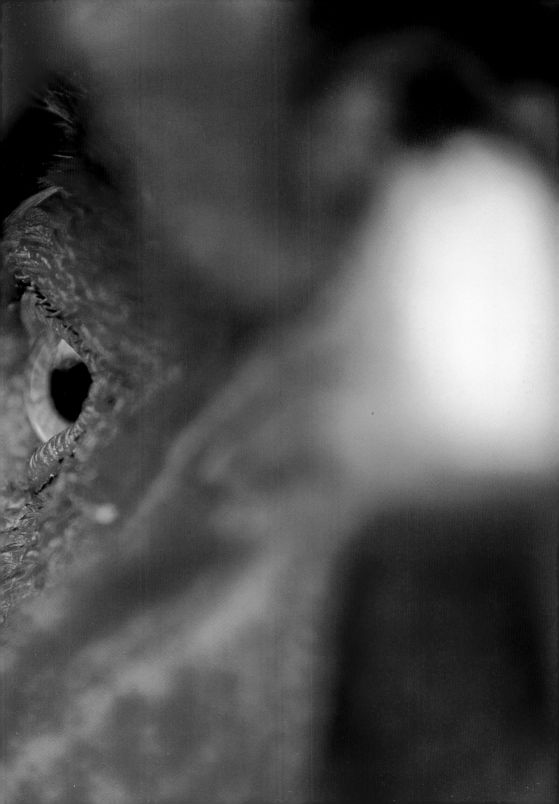

Conclusion

Remember how, at the beginning of this book, I shared the thought that 'without nature we wouldn't survive, yet without us, nature would thrive'? How do those words make you feel now?

I hope that this book has taken you on a journey that has helped you rediscover and strengthen your connection with the natural world – and that you continue on your way, feeling that you truly belong here and are a vital part of it all.

Writing this book has had a huge impact on me. Not only has it consolidated my own existing knowledge but I have discovered so many more reasons why being immersed in nature is good for us.

Ironically, at times it's been difficult to write these pages, as it has meant spending hours in front of a computer screen, which has taken me away from the very thing that I love and that I am writing about. I have found that the precepts mentioned in the introduction have never been more important to me than during this time. I realised quite early on that I needed to strike a sensible balance to achieve my aim in this book while staying happy and healthy myself. It has become all the more obvious to me that I couldn't function to my highest potential and experience lasting wellbeing without nature playing a major part in my life.

Everything about the natural world supports us, enabling us to live our best possible lives and be the best possible version of ourselves. From the seemingly simple act of taking a breath from the air that surrounds us, right through to the medicines we can make that come from so-called 'weeds' growing in our back gardens, to the tiny insects that pollinate the flowers that enable our food to grow – everything comes back to the natural world.

Scientific evidence shows just how greatly the natural world benefits us, how interconnected we are and how beneficial it is for us to be in a natural environment. And yet if we look deep within ourselves, I think there is more than this: there is an instinctive knowing that runs in our cells, our very DNA, a feeling that we are born with – that just knows that nature is where we belong.

The planet we inhabit holds us in an embrace, from the space above our heads through to the tiniest creature that walks the planet; everything around us is interlinked in a complex web. All life is vitally important and precious.

Nature is a wonder that we may never fully understand, nor do I think that we need to: it invites us to be curious but we need to remember to be respectful. We humans seem to be driven to control and own everything we see, to mould and shape everything to suit the way we want it to be. However, the natural world is not designed to be treated like that. The knock-on effects of our destructive behaviours are becoming increasingly obvious and we are sadly and slowly destroying our own habitat. With this act, every living creature is placed at risk – and that includes us.

We live in a time when life has never been more chaotic, people have never been busier and technology is increasingly governing our existence. A balance needs to be struck. All around the world, natural disasters are reminding us that we need to look after our planet; we need to reconnect with it and to live in harmony with all living beings.

The next time you walk barefoot across the grass or sand, or gaze into the blue sky on a sunny day, perhaps share some gratitude for the pleasures and delights that surround you.

Magic really is all around us – if we take the time to notice.

REMEDY

Now that you have come to the end of this book, I invite you to
revisit the journal prompts that were offered in the introduction:

HOW AWARE ARE YOU OF NATURE IN YOUR LIFE?

· ·

HOW MUCH TIME DO YOU SPEND OUTDOORS?

· ·

WHAT ARE YOUR THOUGHTS AND FEELINGS ABOUT THE
NATURAL WORLD AND WHERE DOES IT SIT IN YOUR LIFE?

· ·

· ·

WHAT IS YOUR HABITAT?

· ·

HOW DO YOUR ANSWERS DIFFER FROM THE
ANSWERS IN THE INTRODUCTION?

· ·

· ·

WHAT IMPACT HAS THE KNOWLEDGE IN
THIS BOOK HAD ON YOUR LIFE?

· ·

· ·

Acknowledgements

Acknowledgements

I have many people to whom I want to say thank you and acknowledge here, not only people who are in my life today, but people who, over the years, have had some kind of impact on my life and my connection with the natural world. These can range from the most important people in my life, to the person I may have met while walking the dog and who just happened to say something to make me stop and think: I may not even know your name but to each and every one of you, please know I am very grateful.

My family are important to me and deserve so much more than words of thanks and a mention in a book, especially my mum and dad for being so supportive, loving and patient and for introducing me to the natural world as a small girl.

My children – Owen, Freya, Elliot and Lilith – for being everything to me, each so special in their own unique way and teaching me life lessons every single day; Freya with her wise head on her shoulders and for being a best friend as well as a daughter of whom I am very proud.

To Terence, my love, for your love and support, for keeping me grounded – and I am so grateful you are ginger.

To all my extended family, both here and the departed, who have supported, taught and nurtured me: thank you, I love you all.

My pets, my babies, the fluffy, the feathered, the scratty, the shelled, the daft, and the absent ones – you keep me sane.

My oldest and dearest friend Jay. Jay, I am so grateful that we have walked our life paths together, skipping merrily hand in hand – apart from that time in Morocco.

Dear friends: Mod, Fiona and Paul, Ken and Maren, Shauny, Marie, Mo, Chris, Ted and Bob, Nick F, The Padre, Rev Ian and Linda, Pete, Toby, S.P.A.R, SB, John L, Jayne A, Lesley M, Katie Hacker, Steve B, Damian and Aimee, Neil B and the Wallers, Deb, Jen… if I've missed anyone out, please know it's not intentional and I am sorry.

Kelly, aka, Yorkshire Yogi, for making me brave, joining me and inspiring my journey.

Martine Moorby, for being the greatest teacher and guide and introducing me to a circle that I know will always have my back.

My adopted godmother, Sandra, you are amazing.

To Liz Ware and her amazing Silent Space for inspiring me and so many others in all that you do and believe in.

To Horticap, Big Phil and the students for inspiring life in general: this is the place where I feel my journey began and for that alone I will always be grateful.

The late Sir John Ropner for leaving such a legacy and being an inspirational tree planter for future generations; and to his wonderful wife Lady R for all that you have done and all that you still do; and of course to Thorp Perrow Arboretum for being the magical place that I know and love so much.

To Gordon Simpson for teaching me that every mushroom is edible but some only once.

Help for Heroes – for everything that you do to help those that need it.

To all my fellow forest bathers and lovers of nature, keep that connection alive.

To all my fellow plantsmen and -women, all those with the dirty fingernails, you really do have the greatest jobs.

To Nick and the team at the Harrogate Flower Show and all the garden teams I have met at the various flower shows I have worked at, you are all amazing.

The Woodland Trust for all the passionate people I have met there and for planting lots of trees.

All the people who I have worked with in different capacities over the years: I thank you all for giving me opportunities, help, friendships and fun, knowledge, experience and life lessons.

Thank you to Caroline Chapman for her sound advice and knowledge and pointing me in the right direction.

To Peter Fiennes for being on the same page.

I would like to thank Lisa Milton for sending me that message on Twitter that day and Rachel Kenny for taking the time to believe in me.

Sue Lascelles, for nurturing my beliefs, loving nature and checking my spellings.

Nira Begum and all the team at HarperCollins for being patient with me and for producing and publishing fabulous books.

Finally, I must not forget the most important thing of all, the things that we must not take for granted and the things that give us life: the weather, the air, the plants, the trees, the animals – thanks to the planet for supporting not just me but each and every one of us.

Thanks to life.

Notes

THE SKY & THE EARTH

1. tandfonline.com/doi/pdf/10.1080/20797222.2 006.11433911

2. livescience.com/21275-color-red-blue-sci-entists.html

3. cloudappreciationsociety.org

4. bbc.co.uk/news/magazine-21537988

5. abyss.uoregon.edu/~js/glossary/stone-henge.html

6. gardeningbythemoon.com/moon-phase-gardening/

7. nhm.ac.uk/discover/are-we-really-made-of-stardust.html

8. uk.thenightsky.com

9. earthhour.org

10. masaru-emoto.net

11. jech.bmj.com/content/66/7/e17

12. permaculture.co.uk/articles/soil-helps-depression

13. jfootankleres.biomedcentral.com/articles/10.1186/s13047-018-0285-y

TREES

14. iucnredlist.org/species/202914/122961065

15. nrs.fs.fed.us/units/urban/local-resources/downloads/Tree_Air_Qual.pdf

16. blog.globalforestwatch.org/data-and-research

17. https://www.greatgreenwall.org/about-great-green-wall

18. naturedetectives.woodlandtrust.org.uk/nature-detectives/

19. adfg.alaska.gov/index.cfm?adfg=wildlifenews.view_article&articles_id=407

20. smithsonianmag.com/science-nature/the-whis-pering-trees-180968084/

21. Jacqueline Memory Patterson, *Tree Wisdom: the definitive guidebook to the myth, folklore and healing power of trees*, Thorsons, 2011

22. commonground.org.uk/tree-dressing-day/

23. ancientcraft.co.uk/Archaeology/stone-age/stoneage_food.html

SEASONS & WEATHER

24. curiosity.com/topics/why-bangla-desh-has-six-seasons-instead-of-four-curiosity

25. pnas.org/content/early/2016/02/04/1518129113

26. sensing.konicaminolta.us/blog/do-the-seasons-affect-how-we-perceive-color/

27. cam.ac.uk/research/news/seasonal-im-munity-activity-of-thousands-of-genes-dif-fers-from-winter-to-summer

28. bbc.co.uk/earth/story/20151203-here-are-all-the-reasons-you-cant-hibernate-in-winter

29. bbc.com/future/article/20140505-secrets-be-hind-the-big-sleep

30. mind.org.uk/information-support/types-of-mental-health-problems/seasonal-affective-disor-der-sad/causes/?o=9241#.XcwaKS2cbPA

31. insideclimatenews.org/news/31102018/jet-stream-climate-change-study-extreme-weath-er-arctic-amplification-temperature

32. bbc.co.uk/climate/impact/gulf_stream.shtml

33. climate.ncsu.edu/edu/ElNino

34. climate.ncsu.edu/edu/LaNina

35. metoffice.gov.uk/weather/learn-about/climate-and-climate-change/climate-change/impacts/infographic-breakdown/impacts-of-climate-change-in-the-uk

36. weathertree.com

37. thepsychologist.bps.org.uk/weath-er-and-behaviour

PLANTS

38. kremp.com/plant-evolution-timeline

39. telegraph.co.uk/news/science/11467685/Humans-may-have-evolved-with-genes-from-plants-study-finds.html

40. wqpmag.com/making-most-moss

41. aspenpublicradio.org/post/moss-serves-natural-filter-arc-pool

42. botanical.com/botanical/mgmh/m/mossph54.html

43. articles.earthlingshandbook.org/2012/11/29/sphagnum-moss-diapers/

44. anbg.gov.au/lichen/lichens-people.html

45. sciencedaily.com/releases/2012/10/121009102003.htm

46. zengreentea.com.au/matcha-parkinsons-alzheimers/

47. tc.pbs.org/wgbh/nova/julian/media/lrk-disp-plantmedicines.pdf

48. asmalldoseoftoxicology.org/papyrus

49. healthline.com/nutrition/11-proven-health-benefits-of-garlic

50. ncbi.nlm.nih.gov/pmc/articles/PMC4896895/

51. Always take veterinary advice when treating pets, as some human foods (such as onion and grapes for dogs) and treatments can be poisonous for them.

52. healthline.com/nutrition/echinacea#benefits

53. hartley-botanic.co.uk/magazine/a-history-of-the-english-glasshouse/

54. rhs.org.uk/advice/profile?PID=949

55. horticap.org

56. thrive.org.uk

57. yorkshireinbloom.co.uk

58. bbc.com/future/article/20190425-plant-blindness-what-we-lose-with-nature-deficit-disorder

59. tandfonline.com/doi/pdf/10.3108/beej.17.2

BIRDS, ANIMALS & INSECTS

60. 'Sea sponge could be the first animal on Earth', YouTube, 22 February 2016. youtube.com/watch?v=cKfNVYCu6Us

61. tolweb.org/treehouses/?treehouse_id=3431

62. telegraph.co.uk/news/2017/08/12/many-jellyfish-sea-blame-wind-farms-gas-platforms/

63. listverse.com/2018/01/20/10-fascinating-uses-for-jellyfish/

64. theguardian.com/science/2014/sep/30/octopus-camouflage-military-cephalopod-change-colour

65. sci.waikato.ac.nz/evolution/AnimalEvolution.shtml; https://www.newscientist.com/article/dn17453-timeline-the-evolution-of-life/

66. uk.whales.org/about/marinemammalcenter.org/what-we-do/rescue/marine-mammal-protection-act.html

67. uk.whales.org/2012/08/14/we-are-not-alone-scientists-conclude-whales-dolphins-and-many-other-species-are-conscious/

68. rspb.org.uk/our-work/our-positions-and-casework/our-positions/species/beaver-reintroduction-in-the-uk/

69. yellowstonepark.com/things-to-do/wolf-reintroduction-changes-ecosystem

70. rewildingbritain.org.uk/rewilding/reintroductions/wolf

71. wildplace.org.uk/bear-wood-appeal

72. australianmuseum.net.au/learn/science/human-evolution/humans-are-apes-great-apes/

73. theguardian.com/environment/2017/jan/18/over-half-of-worlds-wild-primate-species-face-extinction-report-reveals

74. nbn.org.uk/stateofnature2019/

75. wildlifetrusts.org/where_to_see_red_squirrels

76. hare-preservation-trust.com

77. hedgehogstreet.org/about-our-hedgehog-street-campaign/ hedgehogstreet.org/help-hedgehogs/hedgehog-homes/

78. wildlifetrusts.org/identify-tracks

79. nature.com/scitable/knowledge/library/
     evidence-for-meat-eating-by-early-hu-
     mans-103874273/

80. sciencedaily.com/
     releases/2014/07/140730093833.htm

81. sciencedirect.com/science/article/pii/
     S0305440318300049

82. dogsforgood.org

83. horseback.org.uk

84. nidderdalellamas.org/parties-and-services/
     llama-therapy/

85. cdc.gov/healthypets/health-benefits/index.html

86. popularmechanics.com/technology/gear/
     a8801/bird-brained-bike-helmet-coming-this-
     summer-15253324/

87. exeter.ac.uk/news/research/
     title_281065_en.html

88. rspb.org.uk/get-involved/activities/
     birdwatch/?source=BWLITH0309&chan-
     nel=paidsearch&source=BWLITH0309&&g-
     clid=EAIaIQobChMI55blyNKK5wIVRrTtCh-
     0g6gsnEAAYASAAEgK19PD_BwE

89. naturettl.com/bird-watching-boosts-men-
     tal-health/

90. bbc.co.uk/news/magazine-22298779

91. birdlife.org/worldwide/news/why-we-need-
     birds-far-more-they-need-us

92. royensoc.co.uk/insect-classification

93. bbc.co.uk/news/science-environment-47698294

94. butterfly-conservation.org/sites/default/files/
     soukb-2015.pdf

95. butterfly-conservation.org/how-you-can-help

96. mnn.com/earth-matters/animals/blogs/
     wild-wolves-hyenas-form-unlikely-friendship

97. worldwildlife.org/pages/living-plan-
     et-report-2018

98. wwf.org.uk/updates/living-planet-report-2018

Index

Photography